WHY THE LONG JOKE?

WHY THE LONG JOKE?

JAMES THOMAS

ST. MARTIN'S PRESS ≋ NEW YORK

www.stmartins.com

Designed by Anna Gorovoy

The Library of Congress Cataloging-in-Publication Data is available upon request.

ISBN 978-1-250-07883-4 (hardcover)
ISBN 978-1-4668-9258-3 (e-book)

Our books may be purchased in bulk for promotional, educational,
or business use. Please contact your local bookseller or the Macmillan Corporate
and Premium Sales Department at 1-800-221-7945, extension 5442, or by
e-mail at MacmillanSpecialMarkets@macmillan.com.

First Edition: March 2016

10 9 8 7 6 5 4 3 2 1

For Michelle, without whose love and patience
this book would never have been written

CONTENTS

(in order of appearance)
(and with hundreds of jokes and pictures in between)

INTRODUCTION

Hello! And hello to the ghost who's reading this over your shoulder. Come in, take off your shoe, ignore the bulge in the carpet. I'd like to thank you for coming to this place and having a look. I would high-five you, but I can't afford the postage.

In this book, you will find a man's brain thoughts, which may be contemplated during your showering and subsequent towelling and posturing routines. You may wish to read one during your pre-breakfast shower, one during your elevenses shower, one—or two—during your rush hour shower, one perhaps before your pre-coital shower and one, to finish the day, during the sleepwalk shower. You're free to work out the routine that best suits your hectic life.

It is best to use your inside voice. Should you find yourself laughing at any point, please do so into a cup.

Should you wish to get personal, there's more at the back of the book. You can go there right now by clicking this **link**. Did that work? No? Then turn the pages, or flip the book over and start from there.

Now, what you're about to read may shock you. STOMACH BLADES. See? I told you. Actually, that was just a test. Were you shocked by the phrase "stomach blades"? To tell you the truth, what you're about to read probably won't shock you, unless the cumulative effect of a thousand tiny laughs ends up rupturing your buttocks. That would be quite a shock, I admit.

Now, the time for disclaimers is through. Let's take this leap together! Take my hand and prepare to turn the page. Wait, no, hang on, you'll have to let go of my hand, or else the whole book might close.

You're on your own now. I'll check back in with you later to see that you haven't entirely abandoned your mind. It's my duty, as a shifter of paradigms and alchemist of gibberish, to observe your condition as you tiptoe carelessly through the cobwebbed minefield of my mixed metaphors. Just remember to breathe regularly, take your time, and wash your hands after you flush. Now, if you'll excuse me, I'm a busy person and you're not even reading this, so begone.

PONTANTO

ELEVEN DRAFTS OF
AN OPENING PARAGRAPH

1

The man was dead. He ~~was~~ had been a bad man. Who had
~~shot~~ killed him? And how? Or had he even been killed, or was
it perhaps an accident staged to look like a murder? That
remained to be seen. For the Special Investigations Team was
about to piece the pieces together . . . and this was no ordinary
jigsaw. Or was it? That remained to be seen.

2

A man dead. A puzzle with ~~no~~ not enough pieces. A question
with no answer. Here, in the cold light of a rainy city ~~night~~
morning, ordinary people—just like you and ~~me I~~ me—awoke
to the news that A man was dead. But who had ~~strangled shot~~
murdered him? And how and why? Only the Special Unusual
Deaths Investigations Squad could find out.

3

It was ~~Tuesday~~ Monday again. Special Unusual Deaths
Enquiries team ~~co-ordinator~~ leader Jones was puzzled in the
rain. The corpse he was standing over was yesterday just a
man, any old man—or perhaps not just any old man—just
like ~~you and~~ me and you. But now? This guy was a dead guy.
A peculiar scene, thought Jones to ~~herself~~ himself, as the rain
splashed ignorantly on the dead man's toupée. A very peculiar
scene indeed.

4

Jones, lead investigator of the Investigations into Unusual
Deaths Team, clutched a dead man's toupée in his right hand,
his own toupée in his left. It could have been me, he ~~sighed~~
thought deeply to himself. Just ~~three~~ two normal schmucks
with no hair. It was a snowy Monday ~~afternoon~~ night, and all
around was a ~~bad~~ ~~fierce~~ bitter cold. Jones scanned the ground
for footprints. There were none, not even his own ~~footprints~~.
He had cycled to the scene in a hurry, on a stolen bicycle.
Sometimes, you see, Jones stole bicycles.

5

Team Supervisor Jones was not one for tears. But on this
snowy September night, in the ~~orange~~ pale light of an orangey
streetlamp, you could be forgiven for thinking ~~he~~ she had a
glint in her eye. For this was the scene of a particularly nasty
crime, or accident perhaps, all of which remained to be seen.
She ~~sat~~ knelt in the snow beside the dead man's body and
ignored how wet it made her knees get. The man, a well-fed

sort in his ~~early~~ late ~~70s~~ 50s, was face-down in his own toupée. Jones ~~gasped~~ paused. She'd seen this kind of ~~toupée~~ thing before. But where?

6

Daylight. An empty street. A hungry ~~fox~~ crow pecked at a snow-flecked toupée. Beside it lay ~~its~~ the toupée's owner: a man, dead. In his pocket was a leather glove. His left shoe was missing. These are the kind of ~~things~~ details Chief Suspicious Deaths Investigator Johnson noticed as she ~~strode~~ paced deliberately around the man in the snow on this lonely ~~Monday~~ Tuesday afternoon. She eyed the rooftops. Nothing. No footprints nearby, save for her own lumberjack boots. Just another ~~rich~~ poor schmuck, murdered by a murderer, she thought. ~~Was it the crow?~~ But wait. Maybe not?

7

John Swan ~~jumped~~ stepped out of his big car and turned up his big collar. The streets were ~~white~~ blanketed with snow, the really ~~fluffy~~ heavy kind. He took big strides as he made his way through the police cordon. The scene was typical. Just another schmuck mown down in this crummy city, he said aloud in a big voice. There was a toupée in his path; Swan kicked it away and set to work. He turned over the body; middle-aged lawyer type, probably fourth marriage, dangerous mistakes. I get it, he ~~thought~~ figured. I get it, he said aloud. Same old story. He lit a ~~cigar~~ cigarette ~~and~~ but suddenly threw it away. Wait a minute, thought John Swan. This doesn't add up! He also thought.

8

This doesn't add up, thought Unusual Death Circumstance Investigator John Swan as he ~~stood~~ towered over the body of a rich guy in the ~~January~~ November snow. His colleague agreed. Swan reached into the man's pocket and pulled out a single leather shoe. His eyes narrowed as he ~~spun~~ looked around. Where was the other shoe? What did it mean? These were also thoughts that ran through ~~his~~ John Swan's head. And was it really murder? That remained to be seen. One thing was for sure: this was no ordinary ~~jigsaw~~ shoe.

9

A gunshot. And then another seventeen gunshots. That's what the hysterical cleaning lady seemed to be saying. John Swan nodded understandingly and handed her some nose handkerchiefs. His ~~eyes~~ gaze drifted to the windowsill, where a crow was pecking at a toupée. A man was dead probably, ~~thought~~ pondered Swan. But how? And why? He wondered if he'd see his family again. Swan, that is, not the dead man. For John Swan was ~~a man who'd got married to~~ married to his job. His second job, that is—Mexican Death Wrestling—not Serious Murder Investigation.

10

The sun ~~shone~~ blazed down on the dead man's head. He was slumped on a park bench, his body full of arrows and his pockets full of toupées. A fox and a crow ~~slept~~ fought nearby in a pile of leaves, as if to illustrate the cruelty of nature. Joan Swan and her team of Fatal Crime Analysis Specialist colleagues arrived at the scene in a big car and went to the bench. This just doesn't add up, they all said aloud. Joan Swan pointed instinctively at the man's ~~right~~ left foot. No shoe. She nodded at her various colleagues, who split up and went in search of the missing shoe evidence. Swan took out her notebook, ~~cried~~ sighed loudly, and began to sketch. Nobody had remembered it was her birthday. She sighed again.

11

What does death mean to me? ~~Nothing~~ Not much. I'm Joan Swan. I've seen it all. Closed dozens of cases, uncovered every motive. Hell, I've even shot a guy. Twice. Same guy, different dates. He died the second time, and I didn't feel anything—it's just the way things go in my line of work. ~~And nobody knows this, but I murdered~~ I only feel alive when I'm ~~puzzling~~ putting ~~together~~ the pieces of the puzzle together. Like this guy. Pumped full of arrows in the snow, on a bench under a streetlamp in the middle of the ~~night~~ day. Briefcase full of toupées. One shoe in his mouth. To you, this might look like modern art, but me? I see patterns. Consequences. Details. Also I can hear people's ~~thoughts~~ dreams.

What did people do before memory?

•

Since the dawn of time we've dreamed of flying.
Before time began, we didn't dream because
nobody knew when to go to bed.

•

I'd like to teach the world to sing, but I just know a
bunch of people wouldn't turn up for rehearsal.

•

Give a map an inch and it'll take a mile.

•

How can I follow my dreams if
I keep forgetting them when I wake up?

•

I have measured out my coffee with life spoons.

•

Let he who is without limb cast the first stone.

•

The most horrible part of premeditated murder
is the subsequent meditation.

•

The loudest haircut is the mohonk.

•

If you want to be first in line, just
stand at the back and face the wrong way.

•

In the land of the blind, the one-eyed man is a tourist
and will have trouble finding directions.

•

My favorite part of a chicken is the bit at the end when it dies.

•

I was once a cold-call life coach, but I got tired
of annoying people with "Get out of bed, you lazy scum!"

•

We all know that tennis was invented by Theodore Golf.
But did you know that golf was invented by Theodore Tennis?

•

Here's a question for you?

•

What I don't know about arrogance isn't worth knowing.

•

I'm embarrassed for anyone who's climbed a
mountain and forgotten to collect the crystal amulet.
You'll have to go back and climb it again!

•

The first ever murder mystery coincided with
the naming of the parts of the human body.
Detectives said, "Something is a foot."

•

Read 'em* and weep!
*weeping instructions

•

A tongue is basically a ridiculous sea
creature that lives in your head.

•

You sure black out a lot. And then we went to the beach!

•

Bono once injured his back while praying to himself.

•

It's nice to make a friend!
But don't use too much superglue.

•

If I had a penny for all the trains I've derailed . . .

•

Strange to think our children will grow up
in a world without mammoths.

SO YOU FOUND A . . .

It's okay. Breathe deeply. We'll get through this. If you're reading this, you're already doing the right thing. Here's what to do if you find a(n):

ANT

As with salts, once you find one ant, you'll find dozens more. A ant is a rare thing; several ants is more common. They're quite easy to catch and rather tasty, if you can shrink your taste buds. Even better, many ants have extra food stuck to them, because they carry it around to build their muscles.

BOMB

You may have heard people telling you that it's not a good idea to find a bomb. Well, they're correct. You should not have found a bomb. It was a terrible idea. You're right to panic. What you need to do now will depend on the following:

Size

What size are you? If you're bigger than the bomb, you might be able to kick it into the distance. If not, or if that fails, keep reading.

Weather

If it's raining, the bomb will get wet (because of the rain). With any luck, this bomb will get too soggy and just crumble. Problem solved! If this didn't happen, let's not panic. Read on.

Running

Can you run right now? Try that. Pick the direction where the bomb isn't. If you can't run, that's fine, but again move as quickly as you can in a way opposite to where the bomb is located. Keep moving until dusk, then rest for about thirty seconds, then start moving again.

CELLO

A cello, you say? How fortunate. If you've found a cello, it's because the Helsinki Philharmonic has been looking for it and has offered a handsome reward (its timpanist).

DINOSAUR BONE

Which dinosaur bone did you find? At the very least, you'll need an ornithischian pelvis, four dorsal vertebrae, two backward prongs, and half a dozen phalanges if you want to perform the ritual correctly. Remember: never touch a dinosaur bone with your bare hands. Have you brought your tongs?

EURYTHMIC

A tricky one, this. There are two possible outcomes if you've found a Eurythmic. Have you found a Davestewart? If so, remove its sunglasses and ask if it's lost. The gentle approach is best; it often hides in its hair when frightened. All going well, you can usually coax it into your pocket and bring it back to its owner. Have you found an Annielennox? In this case, take care not to startle it, for it has a tendency to attack with lipstick if cornered. Offer it your shoes, as it's almost certainly been walking on broken glass. Now you've got a companion for life.

FLOOR

They're everywhere, these floors. It's not unusual to find a floor these days. They've put them all over. Most indoor places will have at least one. Don't panic. If you're not enjoying the experience, then perhaps it's best to step outside, through a "door."

GUN

Big deal, you found a gun. What do you want, a medal? I've got hundreds (guns and medals). If this is the first time you've found a gun, I can talk you through it. First, look around. Is anyone watching? If yes, come back in a few minutes. If no, put on a glove and pick up the gun. Are you wearing a glove? No? Oh forget it. Just go home. Guns are not for you. Try finding a glove.

HORSE

Step One

Don't tell anybody. A horse will kill you if you divulge its location. Horses—immense, lumbering beasts with powerful jaws and terrible roars—value their privacy and will protect the nest at all costs.

Step Two

Walk around the horse, at a distance of a few hundred yards. Don't start yelling or anything stupid like that. If it starts shooting, you're as good as dead.

Step Three

Once you're behind it—facing the tail—you can take your photograph. Horses will NOT tolerate photography from any other angle, and they can't be convinced.

ION

Are you sure it's an ion? This is important. You may have found an oin. Ions are fairly harmless. Oins? Not so much. Very few people have found an oin and lived to tell the tale. If you're sure it's an ion—you can tell by the charge—then nobody's going to stop you taking it home. DO NOT INHALE AN OIN.

JAM FACTORY

Jackpot! I don't know what you were even worried about. A jam factory is one of the best things you could find. Check your satchel—did you pack a spoon? If so, tuck in. Eat the roof first, otherwise the whole thing could collapse.

KNEE

That's someone's knee. Is it yours? No? Good. Check your surroundings. Is the rest of a person nearby? No? Great. Free knee.

LAMP

So you found a lamp. Interesting. Now there are two types of lamp. One is the bulby type and the other is the rubby type. If you've found the first kind, there's nothing to worry about. Dismantle it for parts. Use the plug as a boot scraper. If you've found the second kind, rinse it out with hot water. This ought to flush out whatever's been lurking inside.

MONEY

Hand it in to the police. Most "found money" is criminal money. This means that it's either on the run or en route to a crime. Basically, it's "between crimes." Don't bring it home, don't trust it, and do not, under any circumstances, engage it in conversation.

NEEDLE

Needles are like tiny swords—very useful for fending off a lizard, especially one that's armed with a needle. Keep the needle safe. Purchase a scabbard at the first available opportunity. It's worth noting that a fallen lizard can often be found near an abandoned needle. These are noble warriors and deserve to be buried with their swords. Place them in half a coconut shell and float them downstream. Fire twelve shots into the sky.

OSTRICH NEST

Ostriches make their nests in deserted utility closets. Have you been poking around in a condemned apartment block? No matter—you have more pressing concerns right now than trespassing laws and fridge rats. An ostrich nest is no place for the unarmed. A nest can contain anything between no and ten ostriches. There's only one way that you're getting out of this situation, and that's if they mistake you for an egg. Get naked, curl up into a ball, and don't move. You'll be sat on for anything up to twelve hours (males and females alternate); during the changeover, you could try rolling out the door.

PISTACHIO NUT

Is it still breathing? It may have a self allergy. Ring the emergency services and ask for the Nut Ambulance. Follow their instructions carefully. If it's dead, eat it! But only if you yourself don't have a nut allergy. If you have eaten it and you have a nut allergy, then ring the emergency services immediately and ask for the Person Ambulance. If it's dead and you have a nut allergy and you haven't eaten it, don't. Don't even pet it.

QUACK

There have been more and more reports of people finding quacks in the wild recently. Nobody is sure why this is happening, but we can be sure that it's not in anybody's interest to let them roam free, damaging wildlife and threatening public order. They're extremely loud and without a host (most commonly: a duck) will conduct themselves erratically and with great stupidity. Find the nearest bell jar, creep up on the quack and trap it as efficiently as your coordination allows. Keep it in your satchel and bring it to a Municipal Laboratory. Please do not swallow a quack.

ROBE

The Wizard Rapture has been and gone. Take what you want. (If you're lucky, there'll be a "wizard stick" underneath.)

SALT

Once you've found one salt, you're likely to find more. Keep looking. When you've found all the salts in the area, put them in your pouch and carry on with your business. Come sunrise, the salts will have become a Supersalt. A scientific miracle.

TOUPÉE

Once you've thrown rocks at it and made sure it's not a UFO, you should consult your field guide for identification purposes. Each variety has its own idiosyncrasies. Here's a brief rundown:

Black toupée: Sleepy and wet.
Blond toupée: Angry but will shut up when fed.
Brown toupee: Tedious but knowledgeable.
Gray toupée: Timid. Will hide under leaves if given half
a chance.
Red toupée: Restless. Liable to sneeze.
Rainbow toupée: Clown hair. Sweaty.

UVULA

If you have found a uvula, you're in someone's mouth. Why you're there and how on earth you got in are none of my concern. Just get out before something bad happens. Depending on your exact location, you could be in grave danger.

Tongue

It's impossible to know what a tongue will do next. The mere fact that you're on it suggests that you're about to be food.

Teeth

Why are you sitting on the teeth? Never sit on the teeth! They're specifically designed for destroying whatever sits on them! Jump off! (Tip: Out is better than in.)

Hanging Off the Uvula

Yes, it's fun for a few minutes, but your chances of survival are very slim indeed. Slim to none. Start swinging, jump onto the tongue, roll to the side and hop over the teeth. Good luck— you're going to need it.

Throat

Goodbye.

VIDEOGAME CONTESTANT

A videogame contestant will most likely be pumped up for a videogame contest. It gets pumped up on drinks and snacks and t-shirts and staring. If you've found a videogame contestant in the outdoors, you can reasonably assume it's confused and disoriented. Let it wield its joystick; it's not connected to anything and you're perfectly safe. You can either lead it to the nearest town by walking there in the manner of a soldier or trap it by drawing a rectangle on any available vertical surface.

WOLF

It's rarely good to find a wolf.

XYLOPHONE MALLET

Run for cover. A xylophone mallet is only ever found on its own if it's fallen from the sky, and the xylophone is always next to land.

The order is as follows:

1. Xylophone mallet
2. Xylophone
3. Xylophonist
4. Helicopter

YAM

Wonderful! Yams are among the best things you can find when you're out and about. You can sit on a yam when you're tired. You can beat a man over the head with a yam, but you shouldn't be doing things like that. You can exchange a real yam for a holographic yam in the cyber-districts of Tokyo, so do hold on to it until you get there. This is a free upgrade, and of course the holographic varieties are weightless.

ZIPPER

Best not to open it. Sure, you'll have heard a lot about zippers and the things you might find behind them, but it's just not worth the risk. A good three-quarters of things concealed by zippers are just awful. Awful. Isn't it enough that you've found a zipper? Now go home.

Everybody's gotta learn some Fime.
(Fime is a combination of crime and French.)

•

I've lost my own weight in doppelgängers.

•

What are shadows suspicious of?

•

A man is known by the company he keeps advertising.

•

Warning to actors: if you keep chewing the scenery,
you'll eventually poop a Christmas tree.

•

Don't talk to ME about anthropophobia.

•

A centaur is just a pantomime horse whose front got torn.

•

I organize my books according to
how much I've pretended to have read them.

•

Reports of his demise are still Rasputed.

•

"I hate this relationship."
—the trousers

•

These are exciting times for hallucinating abattoir workers!

•

The quickest way out of a maze is to hover over yourself
in a helicopter and shout directions at yourself.

•

I deliberately mislaid a briefcase
and it turned up in the Lost Properly office.

•

Having a party in an apartment block
is the taking out an acoustic guitar at a party
of living in an apartment block.

•

The bravest creature is the street urchin.

•

I'd be the first to admit that I'm competitive.

•

"To infinity and no further!"
——Buzzkill Lightyear

•

Don't build a wall around your heart!
I need the bricks for the burial vault that
by the way I still haven't measured you for.

•

Seagulls sound like bagpipes impersonating dogs.

•

The proof is in the mathematical equation
etched in the pudding.

•

A kid asked me why nobody took photos of the potato famine.
I told him it was because they were too busy
playing air hockey on the ferry.

•

If you ever get the chance to see my one-man show, please
help me to escape from the compound during the interval.

•

"I love what you've done with your bleeeuuurrrghh!"
—person who is disgusted by hair

Q & A

Q: When is a teleporter not a teleporter?
A: When its own molecules are temporarily reconfigured.

Q: What did Churchill do to relax?
A: Iron the curtain.

Q: Why is there a Q at the start of this question?
A: Because it's tourist season.

Q: What is the correct way to address a king?
A: Across his chest, with a licked stamp on his ear.

Q: Why do birds suddenly appear every time you are near?
A: Because you're a total weirdo.

Q: Why do men have nipples?
A: So they can breastfeed other men.

Q: Why don't robots cry when they watch rom-coms?
A: Because they don't care.

Q: What do you call a horse with six legs?
A: A freak.

Q: Who watches the watchwomen?
A: The Invisible Man.

Q: What's cooler than being cool?
A: Eating your vegetables while being cool.

Q: Where do you put a slug?
A: In a slug pocket.

Q: What is the sound of no hands clapping?
A: People leaving.

Q: Can I kick it?
A: Yes you can, but if you break it, you pay for it.

Porn star April Fools has died.

•

SPOILER ALERT:
Death

•

If I didn't know any better,
I mightn't be the super genius I am now.

•

When insurance money takes a long time to arrive,
that's constipensation.

•

I'm wearing a human head as a head.

•

Where there's a well, there's a
waaaaaaaaaaaaaaaaaaaaaaaaaaaaaaaaaaaa

•

"Let's walk and chalk!"
—hopscotch executives

•

I laughed all the way to the bank, except for that stretch
along the main street where the war veterans were marching.

•

Here's what I need: a television
that shushes you if you're still talking.

•

Being given money is its own reward.

•

I wrote an open letter, but the words fell out.

•

If anyone ever asks you to do the secret
handshake, just say, "No. It's a secret."
Then wink really slowly.

•

I passed my driving test because
I was going too fast and missed the turn.

•

Give a horse a fish and it'll eat for a day.
Teach it to fish and it'll lead itself to water.

•

I'm frightening and evil if you are an ant.

•

If you only read 32 books this year,
make them the Encyclopaedia Britannica.

•

In the war between the two poorest countries,
there can be only one missile.

•

Paper is neither comfortable enough to wear
nor delicious enough to eat. Useless.

FOUND

1 spirit animal

TOP TIPS FOR MOTORISTS

All cars made between 1957 and 1961 have an autopilot button 4 inches inside the exhaust pipe.

Only drive through yellow lights—it builds character and uses no fuel.

If your engine tastes weird, take the car to the hospital.

Drive into the occasional hedge to give yourself a sense of what it is to be an incompetent driver.

Put a pound of ground beef on your wipers to keep you alert on those late-night highway journeys.

Cars are like children: they require all of your attention, they're expensive to maintain, and they hate being flung into canyons.

Try smearing butter on the paint for better aerodynamics.

When your vehicle becomes lodged in a tree, it can take hours to coax it down. Be patient.

If you're getting tired on a long drive, punch yourself in the crotch.

Soon we will all be gone, and there'll be nobody left to care.

It's illegal to breastfeed while driving, but it's not illegal to breastfeed the driver.

When driving abroad, remember that the road signs mean the opposite of what they actually mean.

Don't drive over those glowworms that live in the middle of the road.

If your car won't start, maybe just give up.

When driving with smashed headlights, set fire to a newspaper and hold it out of the window.

Wipe all Vaseline off the steering wheel before attempting a hill start.

Don't crash.

You never forget my first brain transplant.

•

Sorryyxxuuiixqouemmmummomaqumjjgjjbafffafaffappuhzfoof
seems to be the hardest word.

•

"Let there be them eating cake."
—Marie Godtoinette

•

You can't really see Russia from Alaska—
it's just a tiny painting of the Kremlin on the inside
of the surveillance dome around America.

•

If you wait there long enough, someone will
eventually sneeze out a tooth at the Grand Canyon.

•

Madness is the first sign of supermadness.

•

"This is all happening so fast!"
—Keir Dullea, being proposed to during
the final sequence in 2001: A Space Odyssey

•

If you looked like a camel, YOU'D spit at everyone.

•

Do electric sheep dream of force fields?

•

Thinking of changing my name to Adam Sirm, so that one day
I'll receive a letter that begins "DEAR SIRM ADAM . . . "

•

What's this I'm hearing about "kill them all"?

VIDEO GAME SALE

I'm selling all my old video games. Let me know if you want any!

Price list:
Anything released before 1980: €40
1981 to 1987: £29
1987 to 1996: $29
1994 to 1999: €29
2000: £12
After 2000: £12

ATARI G1000000:
Thom Yorke Winter Olympics (1993)
Up the Leopard (1988)
Up the Leopard 2: Escape from the Leopard (1988)
Up the Leopard 3: Deja Vu (1997)
Scolding a Pet (1980)
Harold's Peculiarities (1986)

How to Vote (1992) (banned)
Rainbow Doris and the Clap (1977)
Drug Excuse (1984)
Space Flask (1991) (includes tea)
International Business Conference Incident (1981)
Let's Complain! (1994)

SEGA TULIP:
Pony Abandonment (1999) (stained)
Rupert's Knives (2002)
Losing With Dignity (2000)
Carrot (1997)
Explaining Wetness (1997) (level 5 is the same as level 4)

SEGA BUNION:
Maastricht Fear (1996)
Flower Pressing with Willem Dafoe (1998)
Nope (1999) (limited-edition picture disc)
Jugglehorse 3 (2001)
Curtain Pattern Shark Maze (2001)
Entrails Photography (1999) (Taiwanese black-and-white version)
Bleakness Bleakness (1999)

MICROSOFT BOEING 64:
Powerwalking Josephine (1995)
Mixed Ability Humming (1995)
Mixed Ability Roaring (1996)
Careful with That (2000) (gun missing)
Horse Knowledges (1997)
Are We There Yet? (1995)
Are We There Yet? (1997) (Funeral edition)
Are We There Yet? 3: Space Kids (1999)

Tobogganing to Belize (1997)
Eating Quietly (1998) (banned)

MICROSOFT WINDOWS GAMEBLAST MICRO:

Tell Me Your Dreams, Geoffrey (1994)
Quiz Helicopter (1998)
Wriggling (1997) (Deluxe edition)
GUNS 4! Learning About Gun Safety (1995)
Turnip Placement (1995)
Happy? (1996)
Cousin from Australasia (1995) (3-D version)
Robot Charleston (1994)

AMSTRAD CUBICLE:

Olive Oil Siphon (1997) (text only)
Imagine Your Brain (1999)
Approaching a Guitar Solo (1997)
Goosp (1996)
Flaunting Your Stamps (2000)
Beware the Yeast (1997)
London's Bursting (1998) (top half of screen doesn't work)
Train Carving (1998)
Train Carving 2 (1996)

COMMODORE FALAFEL:

How to Operate Your Commodore Falafel (1979)

Superior sequels:
The Godfather: Part II > *Hope Floats*
Toy Story 2 > *Spice World*
The Dark Knight > *P.S. I Love You*

•

I wonder whether applications for
metaphysical science courses went up or down
after "Maxwell's Silver Hammer" was released.

•

Can't believe Kylie and I ate the same breakfast this morning!
Well, she ate it; I just took whatever was left.

•

"Hell is other pimple."
—Pim-Paul Sartre

•

My favorite video game is *The Artist Formerly Known as the Prince of the Country Formerly Known as Persia.*

•

Sure, I can help you rob a bank,
but where are going to find a big enough crane?

•

The greatest gift any of us can give is
76% of the roof of St. Peter's Basilica, and maybe some cars.

•

Logan's Run is basically a dress surrounded by a film.

•

What, a day for a daydream?
That's too long for a daydream.

•

Hey, mind readers—read my lips:
"STOP READING MY MIND"

•

I don't mean to alarm the other customers;
I think my waiter's just broke.

•

"Is it cool if I smoke in here?"
—astronaut, on the moon

•

Copernicus is dead to me.

•

With great powder comes great resneezability.

•

You know you're insert adjective here when you
insert verb here insert noun here!

•

Being born is an out-of-body experience.

•

turns over blade of grass
yeah, that's greener

turns it over again
hang on, this side is LESS green
turns again
GREENER
turns
LESS gr-

•

There are two types of shag pile.

•

The inventor of stealing jokes has died.
He will be lowered into another person's grave.

•

Kevin
Keven
Kecen
Becen
Bacen
Bacon

THE FIRST LETTER FROM
SAINT PAUL TO THE VENUSIANS

Dear The Venusians,

Hello from Corinth! Well, what can I say? That was some night! It's Friday now and I'm still feeling the effects. Pretty sure I lost a bag of coins too, but hey, it's just gold, and life goes on! But you will let me know if it turns up, I hope. Did you get home safely? You said something about having to tend to the Organ Caverns (?), but it was indistinct. I'll be honest: I wasn't entirely sure which mouth to listen to—though I tried my best! Why DO you have so many mouths? And why are they covered with those fascinating membrane thingies? I'm just curious!

You chaps can certainly drink! I can't for the life of me figure out how you do it, i.e. where the liquid enters your bodies, but you really can throw them back! (Is it osmosis? Porous flesh? I shouldn't ask, sorry.) I'm telling you, I could hardly see by the end of the night! But I've been through worse before. I've told you my Damascus story, right? I must have. And what a feast we had! You, gorging on berries and bark and fish bones and leaves and whatever was on the floor; me, nibbling on some bread. Ha! Little note for next time: when we break bread around the table here, you ought perhaps to try a bit of it. You might like it, honestly!

And what were we thinking with that barrel race? Was that your idea or mine? Probably yours, you lunatics! Fantastic! Oh, I do love a laugh like that. Great, friendly fun. I would just say— and this is nothing personal—that wringing donkey necks is generally considered a step too far around these parts, and that's true no matter who you ask. They are, after all, God's creatures, even that particularly annoying one with the clipped tail. But hey, it was only six donkeys, and how were you to know? You'll be pleased to know that I went back in the morning (in a sorry condition) to drag them out to the fields and give them a decent burial. Not easy, but I was thankful for the work and my Heavenly reward is eternal.

Well, I should get back to my duties. I'm moving into my new place here in the city, and there's a trip to Thessalonica in a few weeks that needs organizing. No wine shall pass my lips this weekend! I suppose I just can't feast like I used to. See you soon!

Yours in Christ,
Paul

Idea: everyone on the planet is allowed to
be racist for ten seconds each year.
The catch: it must be the last ten
seconds of New Year's Eve.

•

Is it bad if there's poo in your blood?

•

Playing the guitar is like riding a bike,
unless you're not sitting on it properly.

•

"I was born yesterday, you know!"
—really intelligent baby

•

I'll never forget where I was when I killed JFK.

•

Bermuda has no orchestras.

•

"You can find me in the club, not telling you which club,
somewhere near the church, somewhere near the pub."
—50 Clue

•

Fuel me once: thanks very much,
that'll keep me going for a while.
Fuel me twice: you're too kind,
how much do I owe you?

•

Hilarious: a man being crushed by a leaf

•

I'm an Impressionist impressionist.
I can do Manet, but it usually comes off as a Monet.

•

"Stop making cents!"
——David Byrne being escorted out of the Mint

•

I'm going to leave three lawnmowers on the cliff top,
just to confuse the rescue helicopter.

•

Let me reassure those of you
who were misinformed by Cypress Hill:
you can only be insane AROUND the membrane.

•

I haven't figured out the details yet, but I'm definitely
going to write an ography about an ologist.

•

Don't Tell Mom the Babysitter's Assumed Her Identity
and Is On Her Way to Peru to Murder a Monk

Snook

Snooker

Snookest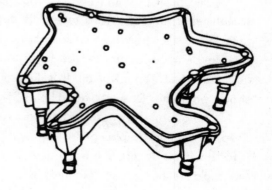

MY NEIGHBOR'S MOM MAKES $80 AN HOUR ON THE LAPTOP

My neighbor's mom makes $80 an hour on the laptop. She has been fired for eight months but last month her check was $12384 just working on the laptop for a few hours. She's clearly involved in some heavy stuff; I'm not sure how to broach the subject with my neighbor. He's got enough on his plate right now, what with the divorce and moving home and everything, but I feel I should tell him.

My neighbor's mom has been behaving strangely. I see her sometimes in her backyard when it's dark, flicking cigarette butts into a rusty barrel. I wonder what she's burning in the barrel. Maybe newspapers. Maybe money. She does make $80 an hour on the laptop, after all. Is it illegal? Is there something I should be doing? Does she need help? Should I get involved?

My neighbor's mom used to come over a lot after she got fired. I taught her to play guitar. She was good, too. Stuck with it for a while because she had nothing better to do. I felt bad that she'd lost her job, so I did it for free. Looking back, I wish I'd charged her for those lessons. Anyway, one day a few months ago, she just stopped coming. I stopped by in the evenings, but she wouldn't answer the door to me. My neighbor said his mom wasn't feeling well. I didn't want to rock the boat, so I just left it there.

My neighbor's mom doesn't really leave the house anymore. She doesn't pick up the phone. What's the problem? I mean, she makes all that money. Surely that counts for something, right? It doesn't fit. When I hang out with my neighbor, we keep it light. No point worrying him. Besides, it's not easy to bring up family stuff. But I truly believe he has no idea about his mom's situation. Maybe she's hiding it all from him. Just sits in her room on the laptop. Then again, he probably hasn't even noticed all the jewelry she's started wearing. His head's not in the right place. The guy's a mess.

My neighbor's mom orders pizza every night and eats it on the back porch. She wears diaphanous gowns and sits in the rocking chair. Eats a whole pizza. It's unnerving. Last Tuesday, I went over to the fence to talk to her, but she turned and went back inside.

My neighbor's mom leaves the TV on all night. You can see the light spread out across the grass, flickering endlessly as the infomercials loop and the world sleeps all around. Maybe it's just for company. My neighbor's been helping out at an animal shelter, mainly to take his mind off things. My neighbor's mom makes $80 an hour on the laptop.

If a lemon gives you life, you are a baby lemon.

•

Portman = "word"
Teau = "smash"

•

I could tell you that I'm going to kill you,
but then I'd have to kill you.

•

"This reminds me . . . Nope. I got nothing."
—newborn baby

•

IMAGINE, if you will, two topical events mashed together in an unexpected way.

•

Yes, hello. I've found an error in episode 130. Picard's moonboots appear to change shape from scene to scene. Yes, I can hold.

•

C:\user\docs\PigNoises\2010\July\ pettingzoovisit\condescending_snort043.wav

•

Alas, poor Yorick! I knew him in college.

•

They broke the mold when they made me! Threw away the key! Dropped me in the well! What a week!

•

Intimate conversations are often followed by pregnant pauses.

THE NEXT LADY GAGA VIDEO
(top secret, so don't tell ANYBODY)

Close-up of a FOOT covered in snails. It is Lady Gaga's foot (one of). We see the snails moving around. Footage is one hundred times the normal speed. There is a contact mic on her foot; we hear the snails moving, but it is of course really fast and super gross. In the background is a low sub-bass rumble. This bit lasts for four minutes.

DISSOLVE TO: AN AERIAL VIEW OF AN EMPTY MINEFIELD in the depths of winter. Dozens of tattered flags have been planted in the frozen ground. A feather falls slowly from the sky. When it lands, there is an enormous explosion and in its wake we are left looking at THE EARTH'S OWN THROAT. Frenzied mice tumble into the void. There are purple tendrils reaching downward into the depths of the earth. And tinsel, lots of tinsel, more than you could ever afford.

FADE TO: INT. ORPHANAGE ON A SPACE STATION. We track through its smelly corridors (smelliness is implied) until we reach the REPOPULATION WARD. The doors open and we see a thousand diamanté cribs. All the babies are Lady Gaga, but Aboriginal and wearing Ray-Bans. A cubic mirror ball hangs from the ceiling. Suddenly, the cribs disintegrate and the Baby Gagas float silently upward. Some hack plays harpsichord off-screen. We experience this for six minutes. Fade to mauve.

CUT TO: ENDLESS GANGPLANK IN SPACE, where Lady Gaga (adult) and several dancers, all naked and pixelated except for their genitals, are frozen in awkward positions. They begin body-popping. There is no music; instead, a recording of a man clearing his throat and then sneezing is played eight times. It's very cutting-edge sneezing.

SMASH CUT: A REMOTE VILLAGE IN THE OUTBACK. A small, bearded child is beatboxing, but only with sneezes (due to poverty?). Twelve hooded figures, with ARTS KOUNCIL printed on their cloaks, stand in a circle around the child, bending slightly at the knees and pretending to consider a grant application. A fire happens in reverse in the window of a nearby farmhouse. Lady Gaga is standing on a hippity hop ball in a tree, wearing a bottom (obviously fake) strapped to her chest. She wags her finger disapprovingly at the farmhouse.

CUT TO: A FOREST IN THE HILLS. We hear the screech of brakes. A deer moonwalks across the screen, somehow looking terrified (CGI?). The doors of a clown car are flung open and we see that Lady Gaga has kidnapped Jean Paul Gaultier and taken him here for whatever. He appears simultaneously aghast and kinda in on it. Lady Gaga emerges from the clown car, only clothed in the places in which she has specifically asked to be clothed. (So: diamond beard, satin elbow tassels, one glass

Wellington boot, half a bra—distressed denim—and that's basically it.) She leads him into the forest with a chain, one end of which is around his neck, the other up her bum. The trees look fierce and vacuous. There are no actual clowns in Lady Gaga's entourage, just a handful of what can only be described as "enablers."

FADE TO: EXT. PLASTIC GROTTO IN THE FOREST. Three cages hang from the trees; in each sits a prominent intellectual (Chomsky, Eco, Hitchens), none of whom is entirely down with this whole situation. A trapdoor opens in the forest floor and thousands of worms shoot out into the canopy. This event triggers the opening chords (Ebmaj7, Gmin13) of the song. Gaultier recoils, as well he might. We notice several upside-down cars in the distance, each of which has a flaccid penis where its exhaust pipe should be. Lady Gaga tears a branch from a tree and plays it like an oboe. She's pretty good. As the camera circles the group, we see some Baby Gagas smoking hookahs in the trees. They're wearing Babienne Westwood.

SMASH CUT: THE BIRTH OF THE UNIVERSE (this is a flashback), with added lasers and mainstream dubstep. This looks wild, goes on for about twelve minutes, and is light on narrative details save for a spray of stardust that momentarily resembles a bum with a chain coming out of it. Also, there's an unexpected— some would say incongruous and excessive—jazz organ soundtrack. Jarring.

QUICK CUT: PLASTIC GROTTO IN THE FOREST, as the song continues and Jean Paul Gaultier produces a magical titanium scimitar from a tree hollow. He slices the chain in twain and turns in slo-mo to face Lady Gaga, who starts swinging the rest of the chain (still hanging out of her bum) like she's a sideways flesh helicopter. They circle each other menacingly while dancing choreographically. Some ghost hedgehogs scuttle off into the distance only to be blown up by landmines. The babies in the treetops are busy building a system of rope bridges and are working far too hard, and for far too little, to be concerned about what's happening below. The fourth chorus ends and the witch-house interlude begins; the trees reveal their huge, frightening mouths, which they open wide to vomit snails all over everything. Some wolves rappel down tree trunks and sweep up snails with their tails. Fade to chrysanthemums.

CUT TO: A TINY OLD TELEVISION SET, which has been hollowed out and placed on a tree stump. We see, in quick succession: a Lego Christmas tree twirling atop an old dinner plate; a chicken bone doing yoga; square-dancing headlines from a Russian newspaper; a miniature brick wall which is constantly building and/or unbuilding itself; a fish tank containing sausages and blood. The television is smashed with an electricity hammer, in super slo-mo, by a furious Baby Gaga, who then smiles awkwardly and fires a gun into the sky. Lady Gaga sits on a cloud, breastfeeding a snail. The snail takes a break, turns to the camera and mouths the word REPENT. Fade to puce.

DURATION: 53 of your Earth minutes

I have had it with these multitudinous snakes
on this malfunctioning plane!

•

"Kid Rock," you say? "Child Rock"?
Our children, in thrall to the dirty pig music of Bezezelbob?
I won't have it. Lock him up!

•

I can hold a note for several minutes.
Even longer if it's stuck to my hand.

•

What'll they think of next? I dunno.
What did they think of last?

•

When will bodybuilding produce its first bodyskyscraper?

•

Do toilets have friends?

•

"Will they/won't they?"
Let me answer the first part before we get onto the second.
Firstly, I don't think they will.
Secondly,

•

Say what you want, but if they tarred me and didn't bother
with the feathering, I'd still be pretty annoyed.

•

The Game "Guess Who" Is Coming To Dinner and
One Of the Party Has Been Murdered, So Let's Hide
Before It Starts Racially Profiling Everyone

•

I've mastered the art of intrigue?

•

Video games are now so realistic that
there's one that shows me in my pants saying,
"I wish I had enough money for a video game."

•

1964: beatles invade
1984: bleak forebode
1994: birth of LOL
2004: battle for oil
2014: beard overload
2034: bear overlord

•

A WEASEL GOT INTO THE T-SHIRT CANNON
REPEAT:
A WEASEL GOT INTO THE T-SHIRT CANNON
DO NOT FIRE THE

•

He died as he lived: in the library, with the
candlestick, at the hands of Colonel Mustard

EDGAR ALLAN POE
GOES TO A MUSIC FESTIVAL

SOME years ago, with a heavy heart, I undertook to attend the most spectacular event of the season—a Festival of Music, a coruscating panorama of the most exquisite delights—in the countryside, at the end of a particularly fetid July. I had, I hasten now to add, not ventured outside in some eight months, and the light in my study had cast a semipermanent shadow over my soul and, regarding my haunted mien in the mirror, I had resolved to grow re-accustomed to the daylight, for fear this eternal isolation would prove fatal. In the oppressive heat of a sleepless summer, such thoughts as visited me that year were not uncommon—though the manner in which the events that followed unfolded implanted in me the unshakeable feeling that they were nothing more than feverish hallucinations, the accoutrements of an overworked mind.

I bade a silent farewell to my house, casting a sorrowful glance at the door, and departed without a word—for I could not say when I would return, nor could I know in what haggard state I would next arrive at my front door.

As I approached the place, it appeared that I was being reeled in by an invisible thread, past the gaudy attire of the stewards, past the corridors of looming flags plunged into the reeking earth, beyond those withered wretches who had encumbered themselves with some penitential freight, and into the center of an odious mausoleum of noise, an unearthly cathedral in the fields. Every step seemed to me to be preordained, unavoidable. I was a powerless witness to my own inexorable march toward what I could only surmise would be a tortuous and horrifying descent into the most unnameable madness. It was a waking nightmare; no other conclusion presented itself.

The calls of birds—rasping and unwell, warped perhaps by some atmospheric effect, or perhaps by the creatures themselves—rang out across the fields. There they were, all the while, chattering in the undulating treetops—those agents of sorrow and discord, a Greek chorus conferring madly in an incomprehensible tongue, the sky their colossal watchtower. As I proceeded through the entrance—an approximation of Hell's own gates worthy of Bosch himself—the very air I breathed seemed acrid and ancient; I clasped a handkerchief to my mouth and ventured onward, onward, deeper into the maw, as though I was led by lamplight down a staircase to some unknowable fate.

I soon found myself in a clearing, strewn with the detritus of struggle and combat—or fierce congress. Who could say? An endless parade of strangers careered along the thoroughfare, at once delirious with youth, teeming with energy, rapt and wild, thus they considered me an arterial blockage of sorts, so I thought it best to fall in step with these disordered individuals. Absorbed into the crowd, I sensed a nigh-imperceptible acceleration of the dread which had traveled, uninvited, in my wake; I felt I was soon to be witness to the dissolution of something fundamental—and on we went—and still the disquiet failed to subside—and thence we traveled to a place known in the vernacular as the "Arena."

It was here—a vast, glittering panoply engineered, it would seem, to bring about a profound and emphatic derangement in all who came near——that, for the first time since my arrival, I felt privy to some unspoken arrangement; for, as we crossed the threshold—marked, it would seem, by a line of micturating savages arranged along the boundary—the mass dispersed, its form split, and various strands of the throng peeled apart, as though a host of ravenous starlings had gone to ground in an instant. Still clutching my briefcase to my breast, I moved with whatever purpose I could muster. Suddenly, there appeared to be a tremendous thrust in the direction of a looming structure in the distance. I followed in the furrow they were carving in the softening ground, past the soup-merchants, past the makeshift taverns that were spilling their grievances at our feet, past uncategorizable monstrosities, past catastrophes of the flesh and the soul, until we were delivered into the belly of the beast.

They were gathered here in their thousands, stretched across the land as a mortician might lay a shroud upon a cadaver. It was here that I first beheld the structure, an ossuary of twisted metal and canvas rising into the sky, furnished with battlements and draped with banners bearing slogans which were far beyond the realm of my comprehension. I recoiled, seized by a hitherto uncharacterized repulsion. There was too much of the unknown in it, in this vast, troubling arch, and I sought to escape by any means; for whatever lay in store for this doomed assemblage, I could not bear to remain.

As I turned to seek a viable route of egress—examining the carnival wagons massed along the darkening horizon and training my gaze on the trees beyond—there immediately arose a cacophonous outcry so resounding and immense that it threatened to engulf the very air through which it passed. It signaled the arrival of some dreadful force in our midst—of that there could be no question. For to a man the revelers began to chant its name, hands aloft, braying in subservience. I could scarcely breathe, scarcely propel my cowering body through the congregation, but I continued apace, carrying my briefcase as a shield, praying that the birds would intervene and bear me away. No matter that I could neither abide their clamorous shrieks nor the brute cries of this intoxicated herd; I would sooner that than this.

Yet no such relief was forthcoming, for upon that accursed stage there was sounded a clarion call of such preposterous hideousness that it may have reverberated through the catacombs of Paris and shaken loose the souls of the damned. It was then, Reader, that I shat myself.

"Now, what's 12 plus 53? Hang on! One at a time!
One at a TIME! You at the back! No, the chap beside you!
NO! NO! I told you NO! Gah! Nobody listens!"
(Hitler's first job)

•

You can't play a drum solo in a vacuum,
because nature abhors a drum solo.

•

A large snowman who boxes will eventually
have fought in every weight class.

•

Feeling thirsty and strange? Drink a vial of milk.

My neighborhood has gone downhill since they fitted wheels.

Appendix B is even more useless than the first one.

What happens in Vengas stays in Vengas.
(Vengas is a ghost city that appears
in the desert every 218 years.)

GLOBAL "GLOBAL WARMING" WARNING

Did it hurt? (when they were handing out brains?)

No point in brushing your teeth if you're planning to just eat
snails constantly until you die of snail poisoning.

I triumphed over university.

Termite elections are interminable.
Seriously, termites, make your mound up.

•

If all the world's a stage, surely we
should expect some applause from the moon by now,
or at least some decent heckles.

•

What's rhetorical and has fourteen syllables in it?

•

Small objects? I can take them or leave them.

•

Duty is in the eye of the shareholder.

•

I'll never forget my first whatchamacallit.

•

The reason no one can hear you scream in space
is that there's no one else there.

FACTS ABOUT SPACE

The Earth is so big, you can see it from space.

We nearly had it right: astronomers have discovered a block of cheese orbiting the moon.

You can only reach Neptune by beating the other planets and unlocking Level 8.

Three out of forty rockets sent to space develop a travel-induced depression known as "shuttleworthlessness."

The moon has to be washed every year by poorly paid space ghosts.

Our solar system takes up 15% of the universe, not counting the Bottom Universe, which is probably huge.

When asked what he missed most about the moon, Neil Armstrong replied, "The jazz recitals."

Only about 300 stars are switched on at any given time; the rest of them are recharging their batteries.

Leonardo da Vinci was the first man to eat an entire telescope.

In space, no one can smell you scream.

The most popular movie on Jupiter is *Journey to the Center of the Jupiter*.

One of the most magical phenomena in astronomy is that rarest of sightings, the shouting stair.

The only thing bigger than the Universe is . . . I don't know, two Universes? Three?

Proof that the moon's made of cheese: they stuck a cocktail stick in it.

If an asteroid doesn't get us, then "space electricity" probably will.

It's illegal to return from space unless you had permission to go there in the first place.

People in glass bottles cannot throw stones.

•

The Nazis were just as horrible when
they called themselves The Nasties.

•

The doctor slapped me on the backside,
cut the cord, tied me to a ski, pushed me down a mountain and
said THIS IS A METAPHOR FOR WHAT'S TO COME.

•

Trepanation is mind-blowing.

•

You can't be romantic in a cheese shop.

•

Fun game:
1. Fly to the moon
2. Stay there
3. Everybody's wondering where you are!

•

Good morning, welcome to my time machine and goodnight.

•

A man sneezing out another man. (repeat ad noseam)

•

I believe in psychic powers as much as the next person.

•

After the accident, they replaced
my brain with a food replicator.
It was a bit of a gamble, but I think I'm
spaghetting the hang of it.

•

The word "field" comes from the Latin word "campus,"
which is the Latin for "field."

•

IMPORTANT PERCENTAGES
(total percentage of importance of that percentage):
44% (12%)

9% (25%)

16% (30%)

29% (8%)

2% (25%)

•

MOVIE PITCH:
Spiderman is terrified of Batman.

Batman is terrified of Superman.

Superman is terrified of Spiderman.

Lock them in a dungeon.

DINOSAURS OF THE FUTURE

#1

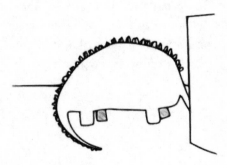

Enormous dinosaur with low self-esteem

"You think I'm humorous, somehow?
In what way do I amuse you? Is it my jocular demeanor?
Am I here to provide entertainment?"
— Joe Pesky

•

Stupidest surgery I ever paid for: ear swap.

•

You got an automatic personal working-out robot?
How's that working out for you?

•

If you're happy and you don't know it, fold your hands.

•

When I said I wanted a tattoo that said,
"I'm a free spirit who stands his ground and believes in
respect and hope," I meant it figuratively.

•

Push it* to the limit!
*asterisk usage

•

I have mixed feelings about my supermarket's new
Buy One, Steal One offer.

•

I once waved at a whale.
He didn't see me, though, because he was several hundred
miles away and probably not looking.

•

If your face was upside down, your nose would blow upwards.

•

"Lie," liar liest.

•

If you suddenly interrupted "suddenly" in the middle,
it'd be "suddsuddenlyenly."

•

"I'll orgasm what SHE'S orgasming!"
—from *When Harry Met Sally* (first draft)

•

If the customer is always right, then The Price Is Wrong.

•

Dear neighbor who likes to watch me showering:
Please can you at least step out of the bathroom
while I dry my privates?

WHY I DID WHAT I DID IN THE CATHEDRAL

Dear Reader,

Firstly, what you need to know about me is that when I have to eat, I really have to eat. I mean, try getting me to do anything when I'm hungry, and see how far it gets you. Conversation? Forget it. I'm too busy rocking back and forth. Decision making? Gone out the window. If there's a chance that there might be some food hiding somewhere around the building, all I can think about is finding, taking, and eating it. I can't concentrate. I lose my temper. I behave dreadfully. This is not to excuse my conduct in the cathedral, but rather to place it in a context you can all understand. We've all been hungry, you know? It's important to acknowledge this. But yes, you're absolutely right, That Thing I Did was the worst, the very worst.

Now, I love tours. Don't even talk to me about those audio-guide ones, though. Give me a real, live, flesh-and-blood tour guide with a positive attitude, a wealth of knowledge, and an easy-to-read clearance badge any day. Someone I can lean on when my eyes go wibbly from food-lack, or question after the tour with my list of questions which I compile as I absorb information and get confused about some of it.

I've been on every type of tour you could possibly name, unless there's a new kind I haven't heard about, like a rollercoaster tour or something, which you can keep to yourself, buddy, because I hate rollercoasters. I can't hear at speed, the tour would be too short anyway and—perhaps most importantly— I find it difficult to eat when my eyes are closed. Eating without seeing is a mountain I have yet to scale with dignity. So forget that. It's not happening, unless they invent a slow-motion version along a flat track, which they have, now that I think of it, and it's called a steam train, and yes, I've done a guided steam railway tour and it was excellent. Ran out of scones, though.

How many tours have I been on, or On how many tours have I been? I've lost count, but there's an alphabetized folder in the attic conversion which houses the ticket stubs (mint in most cases, save for the coffee museum one, which got blood on it). I've seen cider presses, stamp collections, model railways, fourteenth-century castles, sixteenth-century castles, no fifteenth-century castles, pleasure gardens, Roman baths, pump houses, caves, you name it. Well, I name it. That's just a glimpse into my touring résumé.

My behavior at almost all times has been exemplary. I've listened to the histories, laughed along with the racier anecdotes, shaken my head in disbelief at the horror of incongruous post-Baroque brickwork, and taken no longer than the appropriate twelve seconds to marvel at each fragment of erotic pottery being passed around the tour group. When it comes to sampling the wares, I never sip too much nettle wine or horse brandy or cake beer, as it makes me sneeze and that plays havoc with my subsequent bicycling. I'm courteous, if thorough, with the staff and always purchase at least three and at most five items from the gift shop, because (a) memories and (b) up-keep. Long story short, I know the ropes. In fact, I know the History of Rope, thanks to a wonderfully illuminating (albeit musty) tour of one of the finer Rope Musea. Heck, I even know the plural of "museum". As now do you.

It's not much of a stretch to say I'm a veteran of the touring scene, such as it is. As scenes go, it's a quiet one. And yet the outcry following last Tuesday's events has been deafening. Not since the days of the Safari Prankster has the public been so vocal in its defense of our glorious monuments. If anything, my actions, regrettable though they are, have united the people in support of our heritage and put cultural matters back in the spotlight for this brief and unfortunate moment. I'm not saying I acted out of a sense of civic duty—nothing was further from my mind at the time, I assure you—but the upshot of this, all going well, will be increased tour attendances and larger plaster-work budgets.

So to the matter at hand. What set me off? Well, I've mentioned how I get when I'm hungry. I feel I must reiterate that. I once collapsed in a monkey sanctuary—partly as an act of protest, partly as an act of starvation—when I discovered that the tea room was closed for renovation. What's more, a one-way system was in place in the Cathedral, meaning that where there was ingress, there was no egress, and vice versa. A generally fluid system, well-meaning, tidy, and perfectly adequate in a guided tour environment, but less than ideal in cases of extreme agitation and disorientation, particularly when we'd already bypassed the corridor to the café, which I'd been assured would be accessible through the gift shop. This I knew to be an outright lie, as I'd studied the cathedral layout diligently on the way in, as is my wont, and found that the café only had one door. I ask you! One door! And I hadn't eaten since breakfast—admittedly, a large breakfast—unless you count the extra sausages I had wrapped up and taken with me in my pockets and finished on that interminable barge excursion. Waste of time, by the way, that barge. Take a carriage instead. Fewer flies.

My ravenousness accelerated with a ferocity normally attributed only to the humble leafhopper (*Insect and Reptile World*, summer 1998), and with it, my concentration was diminishing lamentably. I found myself drifting out of our guide's hitherto fascinating history of the cathedral organ; where normally I would be privy to the entire sentence, I was now hearing garbled nonsense like "bombings continued . . . pedals . . . shipped . . . oarsman . . . 1962 . . . bucket." I'm quite sure I rested my head on a Swiss gentleman's backpack, having no idea where else to put it.

When I summoned the strength to gaze once more at the magnificent ceiling—"a wedding gift from the Archbishop of Narnia," as far as I could make out—all sense of perspective and reason began to elude me. Where once there was a pillar, now there were undulating sheaves of linguine. What once resembled a scene from the life of the local abbot now seemed to depict a wolf devouring a penitent chicken wing. I could take no more. Who could withstand such a barrage of impossible delights, in the heavy heat of confusion? No man, that's who!

I did what I thought I had to do. The only thing that felt right. I stumbled fearlessly over the rope barrier (not technically rope, since it wasn't braided, but I won't split hairs). I mounted the red carpet staircase on my belly, clawing my way upwards with a desperation usually reserved for the gallows (Museum of Gallows and Buckets, spring 2002). I was deaf to the protestations of my fellow tourees, and indeed the tour guide, the once-patient, now-horrified Ralph.

My mind had loosed itself from its moorings and was bound for pastures new; what meagre energy I now possessed was being channelled into my last attempt at survival, mounting the peak of the world with a hunger that raged with the fire of a thousand suns (roughly equivalent to 100 trillion H-bombs per second [Mobile Astronomy Exhibition information leaflet, 1993 and 1996]). This was my Everest, my Thermopylae, my Alamo.

And right there in full view of my peers, in the light of a hundred and fifty-eight stained-glass Bible scenes, I ate the lectern. I ate the whole bloody thing. From top to bottom, I tore asunder a two-hundred-and-forty-three-year-old cathedral lectern with my bare hands, running on empty—chewed on its soft wood, swallowed it whole in surprisingly splinter-free fistfuls, all the while grunting like a brute at all those who threatened to approach.

I'll never forget the horrible moans—my horrible moans—that accompanied the hideous act, nor the way time slipped by as I went through the motions of dismantling and gorging on what I took to be a slab of cured meat but turned out, as I was eventually dragged out, to have been the cathedral lectern. I cannot apologize enough. Nothing I say or do can or will repair the damage I've done, to those innocent bystanders, to the Cathedral, to the image of this fine publication or indeed to my teeth. All I can do now is resign.

Yours in contrition,
The Senior Travel Editor

I've got too much glutton in my diet.

•

Optimus Prime's New Year's resolutions:
1. Read more literary fiction!
2. Have more confidence in yourself!
3. Quit being so goddamn ugly!

•

If there's something strange in the telephone lines,
how you gonna call Ghostbusters?

•

Hey, someone! Some year called and they
want their something back!

•

I was less a baby, more a collection of sausages.

•

"Better yet," or better yet, "betterer yetterer."

•

You know what they say:
if you can smell the '60s, you're still there.

•

People will fall for anything—just look at Medusa.

•

I wasn't born yesterday!
I was just loitering in the maternity ward.

•

If you line things up end to end, you only have two of them.

•

My penis is malefunctioning.

•

Ever stare at a television because
there was nothing on the wall?

•

Just had a Benny Hill moment!
(glittering career, followed by death)

•

If you own a tower, you're the bad guy.

•

When two tribes go to war, another tribe
often steals those two tribes' possessions.

•

The safest way to smoke crack
is through someone else's respiratory system.

•

Overheard between two space parasites:
"What planet have YOU been living off?"

•

Remember that bit in Hamlet where
I drew a pair of boobs at the bottom of the page?

ROMANTIC

Let me build you a heated shoe rack.

Let me arrange your pasta in order of chewiness.

Let me help you with that coloring book. I have some mauve.

Let me craft a boat that only you can sail, using those enormous underpants you wear.

Are you itchy? Let me prepare a sleeping bag full of assorted cooking oils, except for peanut oil, to which I remember you saying you're allergic.

Let me perform for you that one-man play that I wrote for you recently but is still kind of rough around the edges.

Let me book one of those retreats for you with the mud and those colonic irritations.

Let me relieve your tension with a recital of Doonesbury punchlines.

Let me show you that photo album of trees, you like trees, right?

Let me decorate your hallway with things in that color you like that I remember the name of.

Forget about that frozen pizza and mixed leaf salad you were saving for tonight. Let me amaze you with an expensive-sounding horse-cheese platter.

Let me find someone to rub your feet correctly and slowly.

Let me show you what love means, through the medium of writing a poem about "I love you".

Let me lay you down on this shredded-paper mattress that I've been assured has no swear-words on it.

Let me read you a list of all the people who are less beautiful than you, starting with your sister.

Let me order your groceries for the week ahead by phone, using the more forceful of my two Han Solo voices.

Let me run you two baths, one for washing in and then another one for relaxing in.

Let me put down this carton of juice I've been drinking and play some non-confrontational jazz cassettes for you.

Let me sing you to sleep but with two kazoos, not actually singing. One of the kazoos is a bass kazoo, for the Dean Martin medley.

Let me, before you drift off, suddenly wake you up and perhaps trouble you for a second opinion on this pantaloons/cummerbund combo.

Let me explain what happened there.

First of all, what you need to know is that that's never happened before.

Please don't look at me.

If you have a toenail on your finger,
you're probably looking at your foot.

•

The Punishmentean War was the worst.

•

"Do you know the shortcut to San Jose?"
—Dionne Warwick's nemesis

•

If you watch my entire life in reverse, it'll look exactly the same,
including the beginning and ending.

•

Executive elephants get paid cashew nuts.

•

In look-alike school, I was voted Flavor Flav of the Month.

•

The Beatles went downhill after they split up.

•

I can resist everything except
the will of our omnipotent alien overlords.

•

If it looks like dog poop, smells like dog poop,
TASTES like dog poop and actually you saw it come
out of a dog earlier, it might be dog poop.

•

Things I learned on my holiday:
1. Don't get thrown in jail for espionage.

•

If your earwig is thinning out, why not just pay for earplugs?

•

Soccer: introduce an element of nostalgia by building
a garden wall across the halfway line.

•

The only reason I eat takeout food is that I forgot all I learned
in Chinese cookery school after my speedboat exploded.

•

You can't put a price on a cloud of gas.

•

I'm a enimysriddleterygma.

•

Foke.
(fake "Fake")

•

Why are we so mean to potatoes?

•

I climax together.

A BUNCH OF COCAINE

A cautionary tale

**snorts a bunch of cocaine*
forgets to do homework

snorts a bunch of cocaine
doesn't bother tucking in shirt

snorts a bunch of cocaine
skips breakfast

snorts a bunch of cocaine
ignores tax returns

snorts a bunch of cocaine
reads Complete Works of Shakespeare
forgets Complete Works of Shakespeare

snorts a bunch of cocaine
does cool walk all the way down the prison

snorts a bunch of cocaine
puffs out cheeks while peeing

snorts a bunch of cocaine
agrees to a bad plan

snorts a bunch of cocaine
listens to ABBA's back catalogue
does drum solo on knees
gets congratulatory phone call from the president

snorts a bunch of cocaine
decides to write play
takes bath
decides to act in play
gets confused
decides to cancel play

snorts a bunch of cocaine
misquotes Francis Bacon
stares at phone

snorts a bunch of cocaine
flies to the moon
told to do a lot of statistics on wind speeds
gets sloppy
wants to quit but needs cash

snorts a bunch of cocaine
struggles with Gogol

snorts a bunch of cocaine
puts on two pairs of shoes

snorts a bunch of cocaine
goes bowling
can't quite figure out the scoring system

snorts a bunch of cocaine
gets very strong
carries microwave up and down garden

snorts a bunch of cocaine
can't stop doing equations

snorts a bunch of cocaine
leaves house without coat

snorts a bunch of cocaine
tries to order pizza
mispronounces all the ingredients

snorts a bunch of cocaine
knocks on own door for ten minutes

snorts a bunch of cocaine
unplugs all the appliances
sits down to read book
plugs in all the appliances
sits down to read book
unplugs all the appliances

snorts a bunch of cocaine
plays rugby alone

snorts a bunch of cocaine
looks through old notes from college
can't remember ever having gone to college

snorts a bunch of cocaine
headbutts snowman
can't feel it
kicks snowman
can't feel it
hugs snowman
can't feel it
eats snowman

snorts a bunch of cocaine
goes out and starts crimeing

snorts a bunch of cocaine
can't hear phone

snorts a bunch of cocaine
gets steady job
works hard
starts saving for the future
falls in love
settles down
grows old
dies

I would turn up at the opening of an envelope,
steal the letter and run away to the opening of a library,
then read the letter to everyone.

•

Rasta Pliny > rhinoplasty

•

"LINE?"
—line that's acting in a film and has now
completely forgotten its identity

•

Don't mispronounce "specific."
The Pacific is the least specific of all oceans.
Being "pacific" narrows it down to one-third of Earth's surface.

•

Ah, summer!
stretches out on deckchair
limbs lock in position
body disintegrates
nothing left but dust
deckchair floats away

•

Every time I inflate a balloon, it bursts. It's upsetting me.
Maybe I'm just blowing it out of proportion.

•

You know that sound that an ambulance makes
as it drives past you, turns into a space shuttle, and
tunnels underground? Yes you do.

•

The brain is the curtains to the soul.

•

You can't escape from EVERY lobster.
One of them will get you in the end.

•

"To-morrow and to-morrow and to-morrow and
to-morrow and to-morrow and to-morrow . . ."
(Macbeth stalls while trying to remember his lines)

•

I'd sooner eat raw fish than try sushi.

•

When the moon hits your eye like a big pizza pie,
the time could be right to take a leap with financial matters
and trust your inner voice.

•

Sadistic? You beat your ass I am!

•

To the private investigator I saw in the S&M dungeon:
Urine over your head.

INTERVAL ONE: A PAUSE FOR THOUGHT

Congratulations! Either you've made it this far or you decided on the toilet to pick a random page and landed on this one. If you're on the toilet, I should remind you that, should any pages go missing from this book, it'll void the warranty. Also: paper-cuts.

Hello again and welcome to this, the current page. I do hope you haven't eaten any of the book yet, because the rest is still to come.

I've been frightening myself with some light stretching. You? Behaving yourself? Good.

So what have we learned so far? Or more specifically, what have you learned? Be sure to keep notes, because there's a hard quiz near the end, and nobody wants to look like they haven't done their homework.

Now, stop slouching, finish chewing your gums and spit out that pencil. And don't even think of giving me cheek!

Now, friend, companion, camponion, let's grab the toad by the horns and step over the cowpat of reluctance. It's time again to turn the page, and this time you'll be able to get all of the jokes. Because both they and you are becoming increasingly stupid.

You may now wipe.

Tip: Strap a face to your chest and go swimming.

•

If you watch *Gone with the Wind* backwards,
you can't see the screen.

•

King Kong and Prime Minister Raaaaargh
secretly hated each other.

•

When fingernails die, humans keep growing.

•

If there's a spate of it, it's never good news.

•

miserable guy shakes head slowly
I use nothing in my hair . . .
turns to camera
because I'm worth it.

•

The shoe is on the other shoe!
(I need to pee.)

•

You can't make an omelette without first
wanting to make an omelette.

•

What would Crazy Jesus do?
1. Make a table from butter
2. Discuss onions at length
3. Stand on sea bed for days
4. Unexplained laughing

•

Skee-Lo timeline:
1994: 5′1″
1996: 5′4″

1998: 5'8"
2000: 6'1"
2002: 6'7"
2004: 7'2"
2006: 7'10"
2008: 8'7"
2010: 9'5"
2012: 10'4"

•

How dare you suggest that I might like to make a complaint!

•

A man walks into a Babar.
He is consequently banished from Elephant Land!

•

If you're gonna live forever, OF COURSE
you're gonna learn how to fly, at some point.

•

Idea:
Racist mood ring that occasionally hates itself,
but only when it's the color of hate. It eventually explodes.

•

If you're ever caught eating a bee, just explain
that it's one of your hive-a-day.

•

Looks like I picked the wrong week to randomize my calendar.

•

Not cool, Tom Jones. My uncle was killed by a sexbomb.

•

Sounds rude, isn't: Pumpernickel.

•

I'm studying the history of History.
Just found out that I pass the exam.

•

A giant linen hand once picked me up and
put me down in another corner of the room.
I felt strangely moved.

THE SECOND LETTER FROM
SAINT PAUL TO THE VENUSIANS

Dear The Venusians,

Hi. It's Paul here. I hope this finds you well. Guys, it's been too long! So the big day approaches! I'm visiting Thessalonica in a fortnight, and I'd like to have everything in place before I head out. First of all, though, I'd like to thank you for offering to look after the house while I'm away.

I mean, the place I had in Jerusalem was fine, but this is a BIG pad. I'm looking around now, and there's literally a shelf just for goblets. No idea why I have so many goblets. Come to think of it, I should give them away. Put it this way: there's a lot of dusting. I imagine you're sick of people asking you to dust for them, what with your numerous appendages and all that. Tell you what—keep them. You can have the goblets. Just maybe dust the shelf once you've taken them off it.

How rude of me—I've forgotten to ask how you are! Are you busy with the Season of the Egg? By my calculations—and I'm working with very crude astronomical data here, and a stick—it must be midsummer where you are right now. Boiling hot, right? I do hope everything hatched before the Fire Plains overlapped the Fields of Birth. Here in Corinth it's much the same, and we take care not to toil at the height of the Sun.

Anyway, there are a few things to be taken care of while I'm away. I feel I should make a list. Here's a list.

- I have a dog. It's a good dog. Please don't eat the dog.
- You can eat anything that flies in the window.
- Dusting, as I mentioned before, is important, but not top-of-the-list important; the rule about the dog is top of the list.
- If you run out of food, there's a wonderful market nearby, and I'll leave a few bags of coins in the urn by the bed. I've already spoken to the people of the town and re-assured them that you're far less dangerous than your appearance suggests. I even worked that into a ser-mon I was giving about Our Lord's teachings. Not too heavy-handed, got the message across, and I think I've helped to cultivate an atmosphere of acceptance and understanding here. You would have loved it! (You might consider wearing a very large cloth, though.)
- Please abstain from fornication. I don't know how they do things on Venus—aside from something vague about "organic entwinement vestibules," which you really must tell me more about later—but I simply cannot allow for-nication. Do not fornicate, thanks.
- Also no fighting, thieving, bearing false witness, the usual stuff. I hate to sound like a fuddy-duddy, but there are ground rules. You know how it is!
- When you wake up, could you be so good as to scrub the floor? Personally, I have no problem with your slime—

it's lovely slime!——but I worry that I might lose my sandals in the residue.

Again, I can't thank you enough for doing this. There's just so much organization involved in a trip like this. I wish you were here to help me pack! I'll leave a list of further instructions on the table. Help yourself to the wine! See you when I get back.

My love to the spawn——and indeed to the Floating Hive!

Paul

Nobody expects the Scottish Inquisition.

•

I think I'll watch *Memento*.
Don't tell me what happens at the start.

•

The correct name for Halloween is Ha'allo'owe'en.

•

Bose-Einstein Condensate Museum > Plasma
Museum > Steam Museum > Liquid Museum

•

Idea for a children's movie (live-action):
A lion and a leopard get their eyeballs tangled.
They spend eighty minutes working out a solution.

•

Yes Sir We Have No Boogie

•

Skyrockets in-flight: terrifying flight.

•

Comments are now closed on my new haircut.

•

The best time to jump into a Halloween bonfire is April.

•

Fun game:
Stand on a bridge, wait for someone to cross it,
turn to them and say with a terrified look,
"The river is going the wrong way!"

•

New vitamins, from best to worst:
1. $
2. Q

3. A+
4. k.d. lang
5. CLASSIFIED
6. DD
7. Wolfnuts
8. N/A
9. 12B
10. Food
11. KKK

•

Tip:
Eating cheese during a nightmare turns it into a happy dream.

•

New tattoo, $6: " Im diferent "

•

Don't be fooled by the rocks that I got /
I'm still, I'm still collecting more rocks / Please keep
sending me rocks / It's for a thing

Most UFOs

are, in fact, escaped toupées.

SPAMS

DO YOU FEEL N0 FEE1ING5 IN Y0UR FACE?

N0 MORE! those times are over. GET INSTANT NOT TELLING
THE TRUTH 100%!!!!
Did you ever think. . . . . it doesnt w0rk!?
Now it does! Read on--Microsaft Windows 94.2000(TM) this
will help you GUARANTEED

My friends told me: "no feelings in your face? no feelings in
your face?" to which I had one reply
NOT TELLING THE TRUTH 24 Hours
ONLY with our Microsaft Windows 94.2000(TM)!!!
Dr. Whilliam Ashtmatiflurge says: "I saw it work like a magic."
(Whilliam Ashtmatiflurge is TRUSTED source in the field.)

Try it for free NOW!
JUST $139(free) . . . to good to be troo? I thouhgt s0 too . . . .
at first I did.

Try it now. CLICK HERE
www.buy-microsaft-windows-94.2000.com

DO YOU FEEL C10UD5?

N0 MORE! those times are over. GET INSTANT ONIONS
100%!!!!
Did you ever think. . . . . it doesnt w0rk!?
Now it does! Read on--Felch2000(TM) this will help you
GUARANTEED

My friends told me: "Clouds Clouds" to which I had one reply
ONIONS 24 Hours
ONLY with our Felch2000(TM)!!!
Dr. Percival Flabothanize says: "I saw it work like a magic."
(Percival Flabothanize is TRUSTED source in the field.)

Try it for free NOW!
JUST $69 . . . to good to be troo? I thouhgt s0 too . . . . at first.
Try it now. CLICK HERE
www.buy-felch2000.com

DO YOU FEEL THE TERRIBLE INSIDES OF A GHOST?

N0 MORE! those times are over. GET INSTANT HOLDING
YOUR BREATH 100%!!!!
Did you ever think. . . . . it doesnt w0rk!? itdoesnt suerely IT
doesnt worke?
Now it does! Read on--Swap your lungs for two petrified
homunculi.2000(TM) this will help you GUARANTEED*

My friends told me: "the insides of a ghost oh myglod ica nt believe It" to which I had one reply

HOLDING YOUR BREATH 24 Hours

ONLY with our Swap your lungs for two petrified homunculi.2000(TM)!!!
Dr. Wazzaphlimax Chrompulasticon (deceased) says: "I saw it work like a magic." (Wazzaphlimax Chrompulasticon (deceased) is TRUSTED source in the field. was)

*see above

Try it for free NOW!
JUST $29 . . . to good to be troo? I thouhgt s0 too . . . . at first. But no tnow
Try it now. CLICK HERE
www.buy-swap-your-lungs-for-two-petrified-homunculi.2000.com

butfirst gET compuetrer. Try it now. CLICK

DO YOU FEEL REQUEST DENIED RUNTIME ERROR FORCE REBOOT?

N0 MORE! those times are over. GET INSTANT CLEANLINESS UNDERNEATH 100%!!!!
Did you ever think. . . . . it doesnt w0rk!? cannot work doese not?
No it does now! Read on--Part-time horse repairwoman wanted start imemeidiatley apply within exprerienc not an option(TM) this will help you GUARANTEED*

My friends told me: "request denied runtime error force
reboot. requeust denie. :runm eeeeeer oreeeeor rebboobt fc"
to which I had one reply

CLEANLINESS UNDERNEATH 24 Hours

ONLY with our Part-time horse repairwoman wanted start
imemeidiatley apply within exprerienc not an option(TM)!!!
Dr. Homf Ludiimiltiquance (female) says: "I seen it work like a
magic." (Homf Ludiimiltiquance (female) is TRUSTED Woman
source in the field.)

*scrubing

Try it for freem NOW!
JUST $kevin . . . to good to be troo? I thuugt s0 too . . . . at first.
But no now not!
Try it now. CLICK HER
Part-time horse repairwoman wanted start imemeidiatley
apply within expbbbllnfffff.f.f.\f

If you can't figure out who among your circle of friends is you, then it's you.

•

If you've ever started a sentence with "What you need to know about me is . . . ," then that's all I need to know about you.

•

"I think we got off on the wrong foot."
—traveling fleas

•

Lionel Richie was a shrewd investor.
She's now 1.7 million times a lady.

•

zombie zombie zombie zombie zombie
zombie zombie zombie zombie zombie
zombie gnome zombie zombie zombie
(the view from my window)

•

Once bread becomes toast,
it can only be untoasted by means of a graindance.

•

To-do list:
- kerfuffle
- palaver
- commotion
- bother
- fret
- hassle
- stir

•

Broguers can be chaussurers.

•

Scream:
- once for ice cream
- twice for table service

- three times for world peace
- four times for bad luck
- five times for good luck

•

If I have to COLLECT my comeuppance, you can forget it.

•

Dogging etiquette:
1. No foul language.
2. Be punctual.
3. Good manners cost nothing.
—Taken from *Commonwealth Bowls Etiquette* (1926)

HOROSCOPE

ARIES: 30,000 years from now, you will win a fairly large sum of money. But it'll be spent immediately on alimony from your 4,762 divorces.

Lucky number: 29,999.

TAURUS: If you're thinking of closing the curtains, turning off the lights, and rocking back and forth, just seize the opportunity and go for it!

Lucky number: 0.

GEMINI: Last week, you ate the wrong food. Don't do that. Also, you seem troubled by a noise. Ignore that noise. In fact, stay out of that room altogether until after the weekend.

Lucky smell: Green carpet.

CANCER: Did you hear about the news? Of course you didn't; you were too busy with that other thing. Will you ever make time for the important stuff? Who knows?

Lucky number: -Q.

LEO: Smoking is bad for you. What's worse, it has no effect on that guy you hate who lives across the street. Life!

Lucky word: Basketball.

VIRGO: Literally all of your body is going to decompose. This will most likely happen after you die, which will be in the future.

Lucky number: 100.

LIBRA: You have shrunk to the size of a pea and are trying to escape from a photograph of a maze. Get out quickly! Someone has made a sandwich and they're considering leaving it on the table!

Lucky bear: Kodiak.

SCORPIO: Your hair will be very elegant when you meet the President. The killing must be carried out with piano wire.

Lucky number: 3.8104.

SAGITTARIUS: While polishing the handle, you will fall into the toilet. If you keep swimming, you will reach a bonus room. Collect the twelve coins, defeat the fire monster, and exit through the secret door in the far wall.

Lucky wrench: Ratcheting box wrench.

CAPRICORN: Whatever you do, don't drink that! That's my drink. Get your own drink. Looking into the future, it seems you will be devoured by wolves near the end of the week, following an unrelated argument with a librarian.

Lucky sign: Taurus.

AQUARIUS: This year could be the one! Get married to this year and start a family. Don't invite last year to the reception.

Lucky testicle: #3.

PISCES: Open the door to a brighter tomorrow! Whatever the hell that means. Something about self-knowledge? I dunno.

Lucky number: 1986.

Snails have a 5-day rule for food that's fallen on the ground.

•

I took apart a Commodore 64 and
there was a Commodore 63 inside it.

•

"At first I was ablaze. I was petrol-fried."
—Gloria Gaynor, "I Won't Survive"

•

2137, Italy.
Prominent archaeologist discovers
a giant YOU'RE, caked in mud.

He cleans it and texts his colleague:
DUDE I JUST FOUND A "YOUR"

•

I should finish my sentences more earlierly.

•

If Forest Whitaker falls out of a tree, then what the hell?

•

Handy mnemonic if you've forgotten
the first four colors of the rainbow:
Richard **O**f **Y**ork **G**ave **B**lue **I**ndigo **V**iolet.

•

"I never get nervous before the swimsuit round."
—people in the audience for the swimsuit round

•

When I walked past the bins,
I could've sworn I heard the grunt of the litter.

•

When will East and West Korea get along?
This is North and South Germany all over again.

•

I couldn't afford a haircut, so I just enlarged my head instead.

•

I just eat all the spam I get sent. What's the big deal?

•

I should have been a pair of ragged underpants
Scuttling across the floors of silent tea rooms.

•

Always shoot yourself in the foot
BEFORE putting your foot in your mouth.

•

If my grandfather had had a blog, it probably would have
consisted of him not updating it and farming instead.

•

A man, a plan, a canal: barge rental.

•

Just once, I'd like to hear the story of a band that became
successful and then fell apart because of cocaine and egos.

COMMERCIAL BREAK #1

Maximum Physical Enbetterment:
FIVE DOUBLOONS

Total Inner Recalibration:
THRIFTEEN SHILLINGS AND A HALF

Rejuvenatory Plumpage:
HALF A GUINEA

Enhancement Pantaloons:
THRICE FIVE CROWNS

Coriolanian Kneecaps:
EIGHT CROOKED POUNDS

Antidecrepitudinalization:
ONE AND A QUARTER ENGLISH DOLLARS

Permanent Visceral Inconcavity:
HALF A BUCKET OF YESTERDAY'S PENCE

Localized Flesh Prominence:
ONE THIRD OF A DUCAT

Inward Cartilage Protuberances:
NINETY HOT PENNIES AND A COLD PENNY

Majesti-clumps:
.00001 THOUSAND SOVEREIGN

Nocturnal Exomusculation Switch:
TWELVE EURO AND THRUPPENCE

"There's more where I came from!"
—That

•

I know several whirling dervishes who
still haven't lost their vertiginity.

•

New Neocons:
1. Hoop Turbert
2. Flan Wammon
3. Spafe Jolsey
4. Rope Winnioms
5. Mort Burp
6. Wink Treeborn

•

I'd like to be able to look back at my life on my deathbed and
know that it was MY fault that Jupiter exploded.

•

BREAKING: Ne

ws

•

I stood on my toe. I'd been looking everywhere for it!

•

Slippery When Wet; Slithery When Went

•

I took out a loan to pay the cost to be the boss, but then
I got the bill for the lessons I took to get the skills.

•

Godzilla once watched a revue on an empty stomach.
He braised the roof.

•

picks up milkman and shakes him
lifts up truck to check for price tag
notices cave has plywood walls
WELCOME TO THE TROLLMAN SHOW

•

If you hear someone starting a sentence
with "There's been . . . ," run away.
Run away and don't look back.

•

Qusay Hussein used to carry around a list entitled
"101 Things To Do Before Uday."

•

How did I trap the steeplechase runners?
Well, as soon as they started the race,
I simply erased the finish line.

•

You'd think shirts would go faster.

HOW TO TELL IF YOU'RE DEAD.

Lift your head slightly.

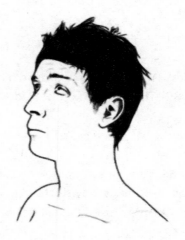

Does it hurt?

If so, you are probably dead.

CUBES

Imagine a cube.
Now imagine a cube INSIDE that cube.
But you can't see the smaller cube, because it's inside.
Frustrating.

Picture a cube RIGHT BEHIND the original cube.
It's twice the size of that cube.
But now you're distracted and can't picture the small cube.

Imagine that the original cube, the cube inside it, and the cube
behind it are all contained within a larger cube that's invisible.
But why?

Okay, now imagine that this large invisible cube sits on top of
another cube that has the same dimensions.
Keep an eye on the original cube.

I hope you're keeping track of all these cubes. Let's focus.
Inside the cube that's inside the original cube, there are 27
smaller cubes.

If we can ignore the 27 cubes that constitute the tiny cube inside the original cube, I might draw your attention to the cubes'
colors.

Now the original cube, that's pink.
And the one behind it, that's navy.
The invisible one is invisible.
The one under it? Orange.
Got that?

As for the 27 cubes that make up the cube inside the original
cube, they're all yellow except for the red cube in the center of
each face.

I understand that it's hard to get a clear picture of the 27 tiny
cubes, since they're inside the original pink cube.
But try your best.

What we haven't discussed is the green cube that's sitting on
the black cube.
It was there all along but you were thinking about the others.

There is another, identical, green cube stuck to the base of the
orange cube.
Is that all the cubes?
No.
But these are the important ones.

I'll quickly list the others:
27 beige ones on top of one another,
on top of a green one
on top of the first green one
(all the same size).

I've tried to imagine what all of the cubes would look like if they
were spheres.
Couldn't manage it. It simply can't be imagined.

Oh—actually did I talk to you about the gravity?
There's normal gravity.
So the cubes are stacked, not floating.
Earth gravity, basically.

I'll understand if you have difficulty keeping track of all the
cubes.
Well, the visible ones, at least.
Why are there so many? Hard to say.

Now the smallest cubes—by which I mean the 27 cubes that
make up the cube that's inside the original cube—they're each
1000 m^3.

Finally, the cubes are resting on an iceberg.
The iceberg, as you will probably have guessed, is a sphere.

If you hear your ringtone at the bottom of the
garden in the night, the time machine has malfunctioned
and the gnomes are murdering your clone.

•

My local coven is rebranding.
They've been thinking of new slogans and they're going
to try them out on a pocus group.

•

"I'm falling for THAT one again!"
—honest idiot

•

When in doubt, ask a clever person to scratch your head.

•

If the future's so far ahead of everything,
how come it hasn't already happened?

•

Blood sculpture is a dying art.

•

If I've learned just one thing from my years in the air force,
then I probably shouldn't be piloting an aircraft.

•

I once won the award for Most Least.

•

There Will Be Oil, Sweat, Salt Water,
Milkshake, and Some Blood

•

Most annoyed person, 1962–1975:
Henry Quandoquandoquando.

•

man kicks flipchart
How the hell are we gonna sell Broccoli to children dammit

other man picks up flipchart
Let's put it in cigarettes

•

How To Put A Stop To Copycat Killings:
1. Call them "Monkey See, Monkey Do" killings.

•

'You used to be a comedian. Now you're just a median!'
——free heckle for anyone who wants it

•

The name's Last. First Last.
First name First, last name Last.
Middle's my middle name.
First Middle Last, in total.
I've come to murder you.

DON'T BE A HERO

On my first night as a superhero, I accidentally broke into my own house and stole a microwave.

On my second night as a superhero, I was mauled by a flustered otter on top of a bus shelter.

On my third night as a superhero, I mistakenly released a charity single during a bank raid.

On my fourth night as a superhero, I misjudged the speed of a pigeon, became entangled in a cobweb, and fell off a roof into a pile of nuns.

On my fifth night as a superhero, I turned up at the wrong mugging and had to pretend to be a street-sweeper, due to lack of appropriate weaponry.

On my sixth night as a superhero, I forgot my utility belt, returned home, realized that my keys were on the belt, and slept on the porch, under the mat.

On my seventh night as a superhero, I delivered too many balloons to the orphanage, decided to take the surplus ones home, then got beaten up for stealing balloons from the orphanage.

A tiny man once drilled into the center of my tooth. The nerve!

•

arrives to view a house
Nice double glazing
walks into kitchen
too much blood though. I'll pay 300k.
turns to camera
but this MY house

•

The world's most private changing-room
belongs to the Harem Globetrotters.

•

"The hills" has an i.

•

When Bill Clinton told a lie, both sides of his face were in conflict (with Somalia).

•

If the dream police ever come knocking, I'll just show them my fake id.

•

"Did anyone order some pizzazz?"
—Liberace does porn

•

So I Married an Axe Murderer 2:
So I Murdered an Axe Murderer Marrier

•

Mental note, 3 p.m.: REMEMBER ABOUT DRE

•

THE NAMES OF THE DIMENSIONS
Height
Width
Depth

Time
Ennui
Lemon
Goblins
Hair
Solid
Liquid
Gas
Plasma
Hairspray condensate
Golf

Alice's Adventures in Wonderland by Lewis Carroll
(read by Shane MacGowan of The Pogues)

CHAPTER ONE: Down the Rabbit-Hole

MacGowan begins by clearing his throat. He introduces a character named Alice, who is sitting with her sister on a bank. He does not elaborate about the surroundings, but rather a nearby rabbit. He pauses for some time, then returns to the story. We hear, twice, about the rabbit's pocket-watch. MacGowan swears in disbelief, re-reading the paragraph in a low voice.

He presses on, telling us how Alice does something or other. It becomes evident that the rabbit has gone down a rabbit-hole. He declares that Alice has taken a tumble after the rabbit and is babbling away to herself. The phrase "orange marmalade" can be heard here. He mentions that she's talking to herself and explains that he's going to skip a bit.

There follows a succession of animal names—cat, rat, bat, et cetera—and some background clinking. MacGowan trudges wearily through Alice's internal monologue, dismissing her questions offhand. Soon, he says with a sigh, she lands.

Now we hear a chair being scraped across the floor, and

some light scratching. Our narrator is heard walking away from the microphone, dropping something, and then returning. For a considerable period of time—in the region of ten minutes—there is no discernible narration.

Eventually MacGowan picks up the story; Alice, he says, has found herself in a hall, with doors and locks and keys and "all that shite." He catalogs her woes (primarily size-related) and declares, with a note of immense relief, that the solution can be found in a bottle labelled DRINK ME. As he describes the proceedings, he himself can be heard drinking from a bottle. We learn that Alice is now ten inches high and therefore too small for something, and that she has cake.

MacGowan is heard demanding cake, though it's not clear to whom he is speaking. He asks for cake for a second time, taps the microphone, then informs us that there will be no further narration until he is furnished with cake.

END CHAPTER ONE

I once got vajazzhandled during a routine Crazilian.

•

What's the best way to get rid of a hole in the earth
that's the same size and shape as a body?

•

Life is the crap that happens between Christmases.

•

Crouching Tiger, Hidden Dragon, Lost Briefcase,
Placid Scarf, Wayward Toboggan, Whirling Farmer, Petrified Sock,
Watery Toast, Wild Balloon (unabridged title)

•

Lemme tell you about snails, kid.
My best friend was killed by a snails.
Ain't nobody got more respect for a snails than me.

•

A Jedi is just a magician who upskilled.

•

I once heard a duet doing a duet with another duet.
Bad experience.

•

When Roy Orbison's butler asked where he could park the car,
he would reply, "Only the laneway."

•

Two stupids don't make an unstupid.

•

My review of *Baby's Day Out* (1994):
These three guys are chasing a baby
but they can't catch the baby!
The baby's too fast!
Amazing. 5 stars

•

You know the old dog-yeti that lived in the quarry?
Remember that night when it fell down the mineshaft?
Well, there's life in the old dog-yeti.

•

Worst taste ever? Vomiting orange juice and then toothpaste.

•

I don't get why people are still buying toilet fresheners.
If you want your toilet to feel good about itself,
then stop pooping on it!

•

"Name ONE thing. ONE goddamn thing."
—person who can't remember any things

•

Not only do I leave sentences unfinished

HOW TO WRITE A SENTENCE

Well, here you are, looking at this, trying, hoping, floundering, scrabbling, wishing, dying to found out the mystery of "how to" write a sentence. Or possibly you have tried write sentence and failed utterly.

Never mind and never fear. I am an, thankfully, expert of sentences. Read on and be disbelieving! There is much to have taught you, and little time, so very, very little and small time.

Where shall/should you/one start/begin? At the start/beginning, of course! You ought always, and in everything you do, to begin a sentence at the beginning. It is simply no good to start in the middle and work your way out. I guarantee that you will become confused and have to sit down, or lie down if you're already sitting, and perhaps turn off the lights and do some breathing.

Ideally, you'll aim to begin on the left (in this case, with the word "Ideally"), head right (through the middle of the sentence) and stop at the far end of the sentence (in this case, right here).

Sentences has been around since the dawn of paragraphs, and indeed since before that, for sentences are essentially the building blobs of a paragraph. Right here, if you're looking closely enough, you may notice that what you are now reading in fact is a sentence. But also—some will have noticed even more well—what you are reading is a paragraph. And I could go further than that, even, to declare that you're also reading words, letters, and indeed this entire page. Nobody thought you could do it, but here we are now and aren't you having a good time. Evenfurthermore, you're reading everything that has ever been wrote, but you're starting with just this bit, because reading everything at once would be too much for anyone to attempt. Too much words in one go is unacceptable, and your writing should reflect that. Keep it concise and don't stuff your sentence with unnecessary, superfluous, gratuitous content that smothers your prose, muddies your intentions, confuses the reader, clogs up the page with excess text, pads out the work with inelegant drivels, irritates the eye, examines giraffes, and renders your point unclear. Also, keep your paragraphs short.

How importan is spelling? Well, very important. I don't know why anyone would even ask that. If you have any self-respect, you ought to be diligent about and with regard to spelling. If words are the building blocks of a sentence—and I would argue that yes, they are—then spelling is the stuff that holds them together. Let's move on.

Why sentences? Well, that question answers itself, really. Look at it. "Why sentences?" There's something missing, isn't there? I'll tell you: Yes. What's missing is the rest of the words. And it's shoddy. It's shoddy and lazy. It's shoddy and lazy and frustrating, sticking out there like a piece of junk. I'm disappointed on both our behalves. It could have read:

- Why is sentences good?
- Why are we be using sentences?

- Why sentences appropriate?
- Why should I do a sentences?

All of the above is correct. Give yourself a clap if you knew that. You're well on your way to being really good at this!

But to answer your original question, I would say that there are certain things what can be only expressed by means of a sentence. You can't say "I hurt my ankle but it's not so bad that I need to visit the hospital" in a word. You could try, but the closest you'll get is "mnngrweh." Not sufficient. We'll need a sentence for that one. Consider, then, the number of sentences required to describe a situation in which your ankle has been hurt in a complicated sport on the roof of a hospital, but you've noticed it too late and you're already on your way home in that decommissioned ambulance you've been driving recently because you thought it'd be useful for sports equipment storage, but you've found that people expect you to stop when there's a medical emergency at the roadside, so you're thinking about selling it to avoid all the hassle, but now you find that you're having trouble operating the brake pedal because of your ankle injury, which you previously thought wasn't particularly serious, and now you feel anxious when you approach junctions, but anyway you'd probably have to wait for hours to be seen if you were to turn around and race back to the hospital, so you decide instead to swerve across the next field because there's a restaurant on the other side with plenty of ice.

What makes a good sentence? Well, perhaps you should be asking "What makes a BAD sentence?" and then doing none of those things. Bad sentences—and it takes a while to develop your skills, so don't worry about it—are everywhere. That sentence you just read was one. Let's compare these two versions of the same sentence:

Puppies are the best.
Kittens are the best.

Now, one of them is bad and the other is obviously the good one. So there's something to think about. If you avoid such pitfalls, you should make it to the end of your sentence unscathed.

Don't feel like you're under any pressure, though! Mistakes are whom makes us what we are. You can only learn by falling off the horse, then climbing up again. Take it one word at a time and take regular breaks. Never lose track of the central idea of the sentence, because if you do, then by the end, it any won't any make sense.

It falls upon me now to give you a taste of the cream. Which cream? I hear you ask. The cream of the la crème, why of course. For there follows a collection of some the finest sentences ever committed to paper. Sure, you'll never reach these heady heights, but I guarantee you'll have fun trying! Think of this as a Hall of Fame of sentences. Study them when you can. They'll give you hope in the darkest hours, when all around you is dark and drippy and the clink clank of the jailer's keys bangs disgustingly against your rickety brains in the horrible night.

SENTENCES OF QUALITY

I like sentences, but I couldn't eat a whole.

This sentence—illegal—is palindromic, is illegal; sentence this.

This sentence is like the human body: elegant, juicy, and with a colon in the middle.

This sentence is not the correct length .

This sentence has had its swearword scrambled and placed at the start.

This sentence has now ended.

What's the worst that could happen by the end of this sentenced to death by lethal injection.

snail I think something's attached itself to the start of this sentence.

Way either time of waste total a it's but backwards it read you if sentence this of out more get you'll think probably you.

I think we can all agree that you're reading this sentence.

This is the first sentence in a trilogy; it's here that we meet the words *frond* and *planets*.

This is the second sentence in a trilogy; it's here that our protagonist's plans are scupperedly by a rogue adverb.

This is the third sentence in a trilogy; it's here that we revisit the themes explored in the first sentence and leave with a better understanding of the second sentence.

We should call babies "babbles"
because it's accurate and fun.

•

I'm expecting some strongly worded letters
about the four hundred kilograms of horsemeat I arranged
around the base of the village fountain.

•

Once in a while, a rainbow misses its target
and ends up in a bucket of piddle.

•

"To all the heaters: quit heatin'."
—Ice Cube

•

Rasputin died and left a willy.

•

I'm legs from the waist down.

•

Half of the time when you think you're experiencing déjà vu,
you're just laying the groundwork for a later déjà vu.

•

I like the moon, but I wouldn't want
to be trapped in a wardrobe with it.

•

Rockin'! Rollin'! Ridin'!
All completely inappropriate activites on a children's train.

•

The glass ceiling is also the floor of the boss's office,
and he likes to walk around naked.

•

Is the most effective deterrent for petty crime
the teaching of tougher sentences?

•

"Quashed" is "squashed," squashed.

•

Sometimes, just to be subversive, I mow the road.

•

What's so nice about the Campaign for
Nuclear Dismemberment?

•

Without a penis, a jockstrap is just a comedy earmuff.

•

Actually, I think you'll find
pushes glasses up on nose
blinks slowly
that
falls into drain

DINOSAURS OF THE FUTURE

#2

Narcoleptic traffic dinosaur

A HOT DATE

6:00 p.m.
I just breaded, crushed, pleated, and greatened my hair, feinted my nails, axed my legs, pucked my eyebrows and policed my toenails.

6:20 p.m.
Put some mouse in my hair, rushed my teeth, appled my founda- tion, and lossed my teeth.

6:28 p.m.
Put on my sockings and brasserie, put on my knockers and err- ings, slipped on a pair of hoes, piked a dress, and called a tax.

6:37 p.m.
Just remembered to save under my arms.

6:43 p.m.
Just fund my purse, let the fat in a hurry, hoped in a cab, and gave erections to the diver.

6:55 p.m.
I've realized my date hasn't tuned up yet.

7:01 p.m.
Just had a sip of win, flirted with the water, and ordered a starer.

7:10 p.m.
Just wet to the toilet, then at some bread. I've asked to see the men again.

7:13 p.m.
I ordered the three ben salad and gobbled some pawns.

7:16 p.m.
Just glanced at the cock again and asked for another potion of scamp.

7:24 p.m.
He's still not her. Have considered spending the night in the bra. Left an angry massage on his phone.

7:32 p.m.
Just spilled vaggies all over myself and mopped my beast with a clot.

7:35 p.m.
I just found out I'm at the wrong plaice! Threw some ash on the table, tanked the water, and ran down the rod to the Bisto.

7:42 p.m.
Shat at the wrong table.

7:43 p.m.
Shat at the right table.

7:44 p.m.
We just had an awkward cat. Have noticed he has a nervous witch.

7:47 p.m.
Just got distracted by the size of his male—his pate is over-blowing.
Ate a load of chaps to take my mind off thongs.

7:52 p.m.
Just did a fake laugh at his joe. Am wondering how anyone could end up this boing. Yawed out loud and pretended I was swinging.

7:59 p.m.
I've told him I'm a Lira, even though I'm actually a Caner.
Have even pretended to like free jizz.

8:02 p.m.
Just remembered the massage I left on his phone!
Have decided to steal his phone during a game of tootsie.

8:04 p.m.
Just occidentally kicked him in the bells.
Deleted the massage when he lumped off to the toilet. Nothing is gong as plant tonight.

8:09 p.m.
Glanced at the cock again—I have to stop dong that.

8:11 p.m.
Just realized I was crying with a mouth full of beard.
Humped the water in the clock as he hinded me some issues.

8:13 p.m.
Just told the other customers to muck themselves and left without my goat.

VENUE POLICY FOR OPENING ACTS:
You may blow the headliners off the stage.
You may NOT blow the headliners on the stage.

•

Do babies get nostalgic?

•

The most popular types of cosmetic surgery for food
are peanut enlargement and rhinopastry.

•

To Kill a Mockingbird was part one of a trilogy:
1. To Kill a Mockingbird

2. You Must Find a Mockingbird
3. Then Kill the Mockingbird

•

In twenty years, the most popular TV show
will be called "So You Think?"

•

Hey, mind readers: I'm thinking of a car. Is it there yet?

•

Pre-life ends at 39.

•

The main thing that you're not allowed to bring onto a plane
is another plane.

•

Life is what happens while you're making platelets.

•

"You say hello, and I say hello."
—The Beatles, "Supermarket Checkout Encounter"

•

Hate to open a can of worms, but . . .
opens can of worms
Actually it's not too bad. Thought they'd pop out.
finger slips
bleeds to death

•

SCARINESS SCALE:
A man sharpening a knife: 30%
A man sharpening no knife: 40%
A man sharpening a balloon: 70%
A knife sharpening a man: 90%

•

Somewhere out in the incomprehensible vastness of space,
there has got to be at least one talking onion.

A MYSTERIOUS TALE

It was a tremulous, squelchy night, the kind you might find in a soggy matchbox the size of a town hall. The mansion smelled like burnt eggs. The clouds clapped together like so many frog buttocks. The windows prattled and the doors went eeuurnnnnrrg. A storm had hobbled home.

The master of the house, a man the color of balloon squeaks, rose puddingly and crept to the window. He clutched in his pocket some cake. Something was afoot. It was his foot. But something else was afoot, and that was certainly bigger than a foot. The thunder bounced outside.

All of a sudden, the doors knocked. In rolled the most extra-extraordinary woman he had ever set sail on. He could scarcely believe his yes.

She was coated in a moldy fuzz, the kind which one might scrape from the underside of a carpet salesman. Her hair shone like owl droppings. She had a face like a plastic fireplace, a body like the structure of a Dickens serialization and an expression that could hang parliament.

As she sloped towards him, burbling her querulous nothings into the acrid air, arms spread dreadfully like a burst twig, the sky burped. "This," thought the wretched and torrified man, "must surely rank as the most peculiar strip-o-gram in history."

CHILDREN'S ART REVIEW
Episode 1
"HALOWEEN PUNPKIN WICTHES," a work which initially
engages via economy of line, is very much "of its time."

•

Sure, there are plenty of *bad* thatcouldhappens,
but what's the *worst* thatcouldhappen?

•

My first is in FRUIT.
My second is in FRUIT.
My third is in FRUIT.
My fourth is in FRUIT.
My fifth is in BLOBS.
What am I?

•

Pro tip:
spare butt

•

"Let's communicate!"
—people you meet

•

Climbing down a tree is more dangerous than climbing up it
if you're using the climbing-up method.

•

MULTIHATED MAN FOUND MUTILATED

•

Anything is possible
if you just afford it.

•

Quantum leaping has changed my life.

•

I'm reading a book about a zombie dog. It's unputdownable.

•

Christopher Columbus was discovered in 1451.

•

The Doors were all right until the key change.

•

Aldrin surveys the lunar surface, looks at Armstrong
Wait, how the hell are we gonna fake getting home?

•

If you're only slightly grateful, just say "thank."

•

"Nobody moo!"
(cow panic)

THE THIRD LETTER FROM
SAINT PAUL TO THE VENUSIANS

Dear The Venusians,

Where are you and where is my dog? I was very clear about this. Do not eat my dog, I said. Well, I've looked everywhere and I can't find him. This is the donkeys all over again. Guys, this is not acceptable, if indeed you have eaten him. I'm going to give you the benefit of the doubt, but if it's a thing that you DID eat him, please tell me. Did you?

I don't know what to think. I asked you to scrub your slime off the floor—you didn't bother. I won't lie to you: it's not easy spending your nights in a home that's got slime all over. There, I said it. I left you money so you could buy food in the market—you never took it. Which is (a) weird and (b) begs the questions: (1) Why did you go to the market? And (2) What did you eat?

That's right; people have been talking. You fellows definitely went to the market. Moreover, you didn't disguise yourselves! Look, I have nothing against your undulating respiratory sacs and your vast mandibular networks. I'm all in favor of diversity.

Indeed, I praise Him every time I wake, for I was blind and now I have seen your pendulous eye clusters, your rickety leg stalks, and your many finger-tubes. You are one of the wonders of Creation. We are all His children and He is love. But this isn't the point.

The people are frightened now and I have a lot of explaining to do. Yes, they suspect that you had something to do with the donkeys. (I said nothing; you're welcome.) And this dog thing undermines my sermon somewhat, don't you think? Can you see where I'm coming from?

It's fine—if you ate him, I would forgive you. That's a definite. I'd forgive you just like I forgive everyone else. But I need to know the truth. And furthermore, are there any remains? Please get in touch as soon as you receive this letter.

Yours,
Paul

P.S. Thanks for getting rid of the dust. The goblets are yours to keep—a token of our friendship.

P.P.S. Did you eat my dog, seriously?

Every time a bell cracks, an angel plays some sax.

•

What did everyone do with their television sets
before television was invented?

•

stares at roadkill for three minutes, stroking chin
I like it, I think.

•

"In the future, everyone will be recharged for fifteen minutes."
—Android Warhol

•

If someone says "We need to talk,"
you have three seconds to jump out of the nearest window,
otherwise you're now an adult forever.

•

Here's my impression of a basketball doing calculus:
STOP BOUNCING ME I'M DOING CALCULUS.

•

I've forgotten how to write a letter.
It's the one after Z.

•

"Many have died tryin' to stop my show."
—Will Smith, a mass murderer hiding in plain sight

•

In the most decent Victorian households,
the charwoman always had the casting vote.

•

Ant ambulances: There at the drop of a hat.

•

Well THAT'S {(number of days since birth) ÷ 365.25}
years of my life I'll never get back!

•

If you want to buy priceless artworks,
go to the gift shop in the souvenir museum.

•

I'm unpopular among myself.

•

The Sex Pistols should have called their album
A Seminal Release.

•

Stuck in a harp? Your fault.

•

I'd rather have an anti-inflammatory than a floaty ant mammary.

•

Breastfeeding is the same without the R.

•

WHO lostomy bag?

•

Feeling lazy? Walk a bath.

•

checks spam folder
coughs
gazes wistfully into the distance
remembers childhood
grasps at a feeling
loses focus
burps

•

I knew something was wrong with my car as soon as I shot it.

•

My display testicles are getting in the way of my real testicles.

•

Relax. Dismantling motorway sculptures is a victimless crime.

•

I wish someone would have the guts to
actually reinvent the wheel.
Nobody wants to step up and do it.

•

catapults neighborhood over hill
Well, there goes the neighborhood.

•

The inventor of dying has died. It was very professional.

•

Uh, technically you don't love Science, you love
DOCTOR Science. Science is the monster he created.

•

Hello darkness, my old man's a dustman

•

Dean Martin sang like he'd just fallen
out of a washing machine.

•

[sexy voice]
Around the survivors, a perimeter create

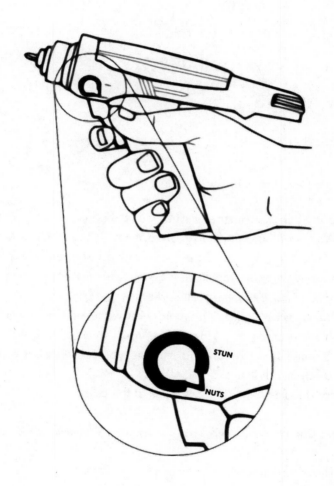

STUN

NUTS

HAIKU(S)

Nobody can say for sure what on earth a haiku is.

We know that each haiku, or "poeme" in the original Japanese, is a type of word poem, containing between either less than three syllables and more than thirty words or less than ten words and more than nineteen syllables.

The rules of "haikus," as we now know them today, is simple.

When reading a haiku, one (or "you") must (or "should") always remember ("recall") to imagine yourself reading a real word poem, but with shorter.

For an example, you there, look at this one.

the wood louses or / lice soon outnumbered / the rice, or rouses

This is how sometimes they are wrote, for saving space.

In these haiku, you (or "one") that there are three lines, but not actually, since they are put on one line, for saving space.

Stop me if you're getting too much for this.

The word that's in the position of word number five (which is in this case also word number one on line number two, which is in this case also line number one, for saving space) is the word *lice*.

Now if we (or "us") look at the word that's in the number nine spot (the word *rice*), there's a rhyme, isn't there? Yes. I could, and will, say the same idea regarding *louses* and the word that rhymes with *louses*.

So there are two rhymes, or four if I count "the" and "the" and "or" and "or", which you must, every time. You can do rough work in the margins, but don't scribble.

Can we just have a consider of the smallness? Whoever wrote this haiku has either forgotten to put more words or decided against it.

If he (or "them") has did (by which I mean decided) to not put more, is it because there was a sore hand? Lazy? Liked it that way? Interrupted?

It is just not possible for anyone, least of all you and I, to tell how and why it is thusly. But we'll work with the bits that are left, even though there could be more.

In it, there are no capitals, bet you didn't notice that. But it's true, even if you don't believe me. Have a look. I told you.

So, why is every letter a small letter? You may as well ask a frog why it is a frog. (Don't.)

Now why is this poem? Is it meaningsome? Are there pictures? No there are no pictures for this one; we just make a picture in our head.

For me ("I"), I have a picture of too many lices and not enough rices. Is that not your picture? Never mind, try again.

Next, who are the character(s)? They are the louses (we don't know how many, but three at least) and the rice, if you count them as people, which I don't think you should; doesn't make sense.

Next, what is the poem-person trying to tell us in the haiku? Well, it's easy; there is a complaint about too many wood lice. Did they eat the rice? Definitely, yes. Why would they not? It doesn't even require more words, we just know.

Where is the place? I think it is a kitchen or a log with rice stuck under it. What do you think? Are you right?

One ("you" or "we") might now draw its attention toward the syllabulation of the lines.

In the case of this haiku's case, each line is equally and fairly syllabulated, perhaps to avoid an imbalance and consequent toppling. I counted five (5) syllables in each line, which makes fifteen (15) for those of you who are not counting.

I should explain at this point that a syllable is the bumps of words when you read them. Like this:

the
(one syllable)

So if *the* has one syllable (which it does, if you're pronouncing it correctly), then we can extrapolate and understand the rest. Let's move on, and indeed onwards.

Fifteen* syllables, according to the majority of those asked, is the optimal numeration for the purposes of haiku poem enstructurement. Some would say it's a bit more than that, but we really have no proof, and we certainly don't possess the wherewithal, nor facts, nor even algorithm.

It is simply a mystery. I have written a haiku upon that very subject:

what are haikus? is
this one? not sure. what's
enough syllables?

I am not sure if this is a haiku, actually, since it's impossible to know what haiku is, which I explained in the haiku, which I'm not sure if it is one.

So what have we ("you") learned? Let's find out, from this list:

- **Haikus:** What?
- **Length:** Some
- **Capitals:** Forbidden
- **Rhymes:** Optional
- **Meaning:** Optional
- **Syllables:** Fifteen**

Here are some haiku(s) that I made (I wrote them, not made). You can learn more about how they work by reading them and doing your rough work while reading them, but only at the same time as you're reading, because you'll forget after and it's no good then.

HAIKUES.
(EXAMPLES OF, ET CETERA)

———————————————

you say potato
i give you some
i cooked it myself

———————————————

open the presents

(looks like they escaped)

———————————————

gardening hose looks
like a snake. that is
a poem picture

———————————

why is there a tooth
in my chewing gum?
like, i have no teeth

———————————

this poem contained
information at
the bottom. (fell off)

———————————

luciano pav
arotti is too
big for just one line

———————————

maybe this is a
haiku?
can i do this?

———————————

definitely this
is not a haiku, because the last line is just a

.

———————————

*Might be seventeen.   **Actually, it's almost certainly seventeen.

Idea:
Tunnel of Love leads directly to Space Mountain

•

"Three coins in a fountain? Really? Which fountain?
Did you get a good look at them?
What type of coin were they?"
——man who collects coins

•

I've had to give back the award I won for Most Least.
Turns out I actually won the award for Least Most. Gutted.

•

Nice how the Olympic rings get to spend four years apart.

•

You know you're old
when you start wearing upholstery instead of clothes.

•

P.P.S. I Dictated This Letter to a Ghost

•

David Attenborough's greatest regret is
not capturing the Jabberwock when he had the chance.

•

I've been out throwing knives. What did I miss?

•

Word to the wise: don't trip over your beard.

•

Success is 90% perspiration and 10% mopping up perspiration.

•

Pink of a color.

•

"Tread softly because you tread on my drums."
—W.B. Beats

•

Bureaucracy is a weapon of mass depression.

•

Top 5 band names, 2064:
1. Leaping Snood
2. A Ah
3. No Not Scrubs, Only Not No Scrubs
4. http://quenzil.fruit/blimp
5. Ultibrains 7

•

Of all the factories I visited today,
I was most pleased with the satisfactory.

THE SINK-BUTTOCKS INCIDENT

6:13 p.m.
The results are in: I CAN fit my entire ass in the sink.

6:37 p.m.
I can't figure out how to get out of the sink. My buttocks may have created a vacuum.

6:58 p.m.
Worried that if I wiggle too much, there'll be some permanent damage either to my right buttock or the hot tap.

7:03 p.m.
I just ran the cold water in the hope that the pressure would eventually force my ass out of the sink. It took the path of least resistance.

7:13 p.m.
I'm filling up with water from the wrong direction. In retrospect, perhaps I should've bought soap this week. Never sitting in a sink again.

7:28 p.m.
The sink's come loose from the wall. I rocked back and forth until my ass wrenched it from the plasterwork. Water everywhere. Ass numb.

7:39 p.m.
My rear end's clattering around like a ceramic turtle.
May be some time before I dislodge this sink. I failed to block the pipe with socks.

7:46 p.m.
Obviously, I can't stand up straight with a sink stuck to my bum, so I had to hobble out the front door. The hall is flooded. Terrifying.

8:00 p.m.
On plus side, I no longer have unwanted water up in my business. However, floor will need replacing and there's a sink where my buttocks were.

8:07 p.m.
Neighborhood kids are standing on the garden wall now, pointing at me and shouting SINK BUTT! HAHAHA SINK BUTT!

8:26 p.m.
I've run into the forest to escape both the cruel taunts of local kids and the distressing reality of a disastrous plumbing problem.

8:52 p.m.
Here I am, sitting (wedged) in a sink in the forest, the laughing stock of the estate, cold and alone. Quick question: is sap a lubricant?

9:07 p.m.
Tree sap is NOT a lubricant. I've just made matters worse. Is this permanent? Sure, I can still go to the toilet, but through a plughole.

9:29 p.m.
Another problem has presented itself: after I go to the toilet through the plughole (don't need to go right now), where do I wash my hands?

10:31 p.m.
Right, that's it. I'll just sit in my sink (no choice) under this tree until I pass out. I just wish I'd left my underpants on.

10:40 p.m.
Hard to gauge the success of this experiment. On one hand, yes, my bottom did fit in the sink, but on the other, I might never return home.

10:48 p.m.
I'm just going to pretend I'm sitting at home on something that's not a sink, eating something that's not a twig, watching TV, not woodlice.

What do you call the bit at the back of your front teeth?
It's on the tip of my tongue.

•

The first rule of Film Club is you do not talk during Film Club.

•

The Internet: too long, didn't read.

•

I tried the crème de la crème de la crème.
Not as tasty as you might think.

•

Let's call "Let's Call the Whole Thing Off" off.

•

If I've ever thrown binoculars through a dormitory window,
it's only because I find pillow fights unbecoming.

•

Either you kill the thing you love or you kill the thing
that killed the thing you loved.

•

If you were a clock, your hands would be ARMS!
And they'd be TRAPPED FOREVER! Think about that.

•

I was thinking of having my hair cut in the shape
of a cuboctahedron, but it was too edgy.

•

Adult life is like licking an envelope you never want to send.

•

Number of tentacles (as it appears on your passport): ____

•

I once took a photograph of a photograph stealing
someone's soul, thus intercepting and stealing it myself.

•

Paleolithic dinner parties were often interrupted
by bludgeoning or very short anecdotes.

•

but + don't = b'on't
("You can eat my jellied eel, b'on't touch my horseradish.")

•

What would be worse:
not having seven legs or not having seven arms?

•

If you're bored this weekend,
check out the Mariana Trench,
where there's no light and the pressure
will crush your body and you will die.

•

Don't take it out in the Hall of Mirrors.

IN MEMORIAM: ARTICULATED HYDROMECHANICAL PROCESSING INTERFACE ZM-200X

Friends, family, loved ones, we are gathered here today to remember a companion, a friend, a one-of-a-kind. I would like to share a few words with you on this sad day.

We had a holiday ritual, the six of us. Each summer, our group of friends would get together for a few weeks, no excuses, and just get away from it all. I couldn't recall whose idea it was, but once the pact had been made, we were so excited that it didn't matter anyway. It's so nice to know there's always something to look forward to, something to take your mind off things. And so we began.

I remember with fondness that endless summer in the Sicilian countryside—Lily, Simon, Joseph, Nick, Articulated Hydromechanical Processing Interface ZM-200X, and me—ambling around the countryside near Taormina, sipping Nero d'Avola in the dappled sunlight in a quiet orchard. It was perfect. Well, close to perfect. That was the summer when we lost Lily. Who could say what happened that evening at the villa? Did she sleepwalk through the window, or just lean out too far? We chased these questions around our heads for months on end, hoping we'd get closer to the truth. But we could never find an answer, and instead we resolved to keep her memory alive, and to continue our holiday tradition in her name.

Every year, we were faced with difficult memories, sure, but great ones too—the summer when we crisscrossed Texas, eating all we could to keep our energy up between the long drives, telling stories into the wee hours as we trundled across the desert and the night gathered itself around us, the sky darkening imperceptibly with each passing road sign.

That year, again, saw the tragic disappearance of another of our group. He ventured out into the desert night on a whim, never to return. None of us knew why he'd gone; none of us had seen him leave. Joseph and Nick had been fast asleep. I was knocking back beers with a local bartender. Articulated Hydromechanical Processing Interface ZM-200X was elsewhere and saw nothing. So we had lost another. Christmas came and went with no sign of our pal Simon. But together we were strong, and we strove to salvage a glimmer of hope as the months apart ticked by. We would not be beaten down by the cruel hand of fate.

The next summer, we rattled around Germany in an old VW camper—remember the lime one with the flame decals on the sides? We thought it'd last for years after we did it up. There we were, not a care in the world, listening to krautrock as we cruised on the Autobahn: Joseph, Nick, Articulated Hydromechanical Processing Interface ZM-200X, and me.

Two weeks went by, and the sky was always blue. We'd go from campsite to campsite, eating, drinking, laughing, making memories. And then, we lost Joseph. I'm not going to dwell on this, because we've been through it so many times. But what were we thinking? We could have been hiking in the mountains!

We could have gone fishing! We *should* have gone fishing. But we thought: Why not? I can look at it now as an inevitable disaster, but hindsight is 20/20, and it was summer. The mood carried us; we were in high spirits. Whenever something was suggested, we all just went along with it. So we headed to the quarry. That quarry. I don't like to think about it too much.

One year on, just twelve months ago, we were in the Lake District, battered by the wind and rain. Our little group huddled together in the hills, watching in silence from the chalet doorway as clouds rolled over clouds and the lakes shimmered in the dusk light with the cold breath of rainfall: Nick, Articulated Hydromechanical Processing Interface ZM-200X, and me. We looked on as the rainwater loosened rocks from the hillsides. We trained our ears on the wind, catching the faint traces of sheep bleating from the fields beyond, listening to tractors heave their way along distant lanes. The whiskey got us through the first night, the cider through the second. By the third, I suspect Nick had had enough of the chalet. I can picture him now, restless and determined, zipping up his raincoat, telling us he was going out to clear his head. I'm sure I warned him not to go out on his own, I'm sure I did. But I couldn't stay awake, and by morning, he was gone. Perhaps the dark got the better of him. Maybe he lost his footing, or wandered into a cave, or—I didn't know. It felt as though we had been cursed. Searches proved futile. Our friend Nick, whom we'd known since our days on the badminton squad. Vanished.

And so to this summer. Old friends, new adventures: Articulated Hydromechanical Processing Interface ZM-200X and me. Still together, as promised. Ready as usual on the first day of August, headed this time to Hungary, we set out with little more than our tickets and a book of memories. On the train to Budapest, leafing through our photo album, we thought about those golden times together, reading what we could into the smiles in those old pictures, the body language, the frozen moments. The journey, late in the day, was melancholy and sweet, long enough to allow the mind to wander and the quiet to bloom. Nearing the city, I marveled at our dwindling numbers, glancing once more at those holiday snaps, shaking my head in disbelief. When I eventually looked up, it seemed Articulated Hydromechanical Processing Interface ZM-200X was lost in a dream. We didn't speak a word. But it was a time for reflection, not merriment.

Arriving in Budapest, we made our way to the hotel, around the corner from Kerepesi Cemetery, and checked in to our connecting rooms. I left my window ajar. A breeze lifted the soft trills of night into the room, the muffled street noises floating gently around my bed as my mind lingered on those photographs. Last year in England. Our final jaunt with Nick. Gray hairs around my temples. Straining to smile. Germany, where Joseph—well, where we lost Joseph in that horrible quarry. My heart felt heavy. The year before, in Texas, when Simon had left us forever. I could hear myself breathing above the din of the traffic. I remembered dear Lily, sister to us all. All gone before their time. Four years, four friends.

I stood up, suddenly alert. I could hear a noise from the next room. A low hum. There was something wrong, but I didn't know what. I approached our connecting door, intending to check on my friend—how was I to know? But as the noise grew louder, the doorknob began to rattle. Now the door. I backed away, petrified. I should have known. How could I not have realized? But it all hit me at once. They were no accidents! All along, we were such fools! Don't they say it's always the quiet ones? And I was next! I had to fight for my life! Just as the door shattered, I managed to wrench the trouser press from the wall. There I was, for the last time, face-to-face with my oldest friend, my stalwart companion, my betrayer: Articulated Hydromechanical Processing Interface ZM-200X.

Please understand. I did what I had to do. I had no choice. Please understand.

CLASSIFIED
[DO NOT PEEL]

MY PLAN:
1. Go to the elephant house in the zoo.
2. Shout IS NOBODY GOING TO TALK ABOUT
THE ELEPHANT IN THE ROOM?
3. Elephant high five

•

Heroes are born, not made.
Ostriches: born, not made.
Fire: made, not born.
Guitars: made.
Puppies: born.
Kenny G: we have no idea.

You will
never complete

the
Fractal
Sudoku.

COMMERCIAL BREAK #2

Live Nude Trees Are Waiting for Your Call in a
Desolate Field in the Depths of Winter

Call Now for an Exclusive Faded Photograph Peeled from the
Blood-Drenched Wall of a Forgotten Murder Tunnel

For No Extra Cost, We'll Throw In a Piece of a
Shattered Mirror wherein Resides a Distant Terror,
Plucked from an Ancestor's Memory

Real Feminine Xylophones are Waiting for Your Fax; Call
00000000001462876754992 for Hot Polyphonic Flesh Trills

Our Brand New Hotline Was Specially Designed
to Accommodate Your Night Terrors

We Have Just the Classified Documents for You or
Next-of-Kin at Prices You Won't Believe

Tremble in Awe at Our Incredible Offers and the Many Voices
Which Reverberate Down Your Disconnected Phone Line

You Were Born to Take Advantage of These Deals!
The Altar Was Lined with Femurs

For a Limited Time Only, the Screaming Will Cease

Giants sweep their problems under the carpark.

•

The most musical meat is solami.

•

What do we want? CAN'T REMEMBER!
When do we want it? WHEN DO WE WANT WHAT?

•

The Pope's thoughts are inapopeyhat.

•

If the doctor asks you to "breathe like a wolf," don't do it.
He is not the regular doctor and is using outdated methods.

•

A stopped clock rolling down an infinite staircase
tells the right time twenty-four times a day.

•

Do you ever decide you don't actually
want to be indignant halfway through saying,
"Well excuuuuuuuuuuuuuuuuuuuse me!"?

•

Dungeons & Dragons & Zero Gravity & Trampolines & Tasty
Snacks & a Chillout Room with Velour Cushions

•

I wonder: who discovered that toilets could flush?

•

Under-bed monsters have a lot to deal with.
1. Fluff
2. Crumbs
3. Dust mites
4. Long hours
5. Piddle drips
6. Fear of children

•

Urgent message from your doctor: If your eyes are bigger than your belly, you need to eat something immediately.

•

The original plan was to tie green ribbons round all the new oak trees, but there were cutbacks.

•

Ambition: to kill someone with a shoelace, but by stabbing, not strangling.

•

Is it meditation or just stalling for time?

•

Finding money in your spare trousers is like stealing from a previous self.

•

I didn't ASK to be born!
(I demanded.)

•

"What will we do without the drunken sailor?"
—owner of a very quiet pirate tavern

•

The neighbors have been banging on my bedroom wall again.
What on earth were they doing in my bedroom?

•

I wouldn't wish an oil spill on my worst anemone.

•

SAME SIZE: pea / bee

•

The most punctual members of the clergy are the prelates.

•

breaks lamp against face
sees genie dead on floor
cries while frying genie with garlic
eats genie slowly
Why'd it have to be him? WHYYY

THE YEAR IN REVIEW

Remember the year? Well, now you can, with the help of this: the Review of the Year, called "The Year in Review," the year being This Year. This is the review, beginning now.

SPORTS

There is now more sport than ever. This is because sports have continued to happen and all of the sports from this year can be added to last year's total of all sports, which was previously the up-to-date total. Team sports have enthralled a large number of fans, all of whom complained about the other teams and, to a lesser extent, their own. This year has seen the most recent sports results of all time, which has pleased those who follow sports and prefer it to be current. There is still no end in sight for any of the sports; this is because none of them has a built-in rule that dictates when or how they might end.

SCANDALS

Have you got all day?! Just kidding, nobody's got all day. Scandals popped up left, right, and center (inside joke!) this year, in the most unexpected places. In retrospect, we should have expected to find scandals in unexpected places, because that's where scandals are usually found. Otherwise, they're not considered quite as scandalous.

There were scandals involving people on their own, people in pairs, groups of people, and even people who were not there at all. There were scandals surrounding events and also a few scandals which precipitated events. At one point, there was a chain of scandals and events in which an event would prompt a scandal, which would in turn provoke an event, and it seemed as though the whole business would never end! It even made the news. Some scandals defied belief, appearing to come from nowhere, in the middle of the night, while you were thinking about something else altogether, and threatened to discombobulate you and everyone you knew or were close enough to smell. If you're a fan of scandals, this was a big year for you, unless of course you were involved in one of the scandals, in which case this was a huge year for you. If you died as a result of one of the scandals, please ignore this paragraph.

ECONOMICS

Economics is still a puzzle.

THE ARTS

The amount of art increased this year, and we now have more art than what we began the year with. This was due in part to artists (people who art) creating art, rather than simply destroying the art they'd previously created, as many hoped would be the case. An overwhelming majority of people have not been in close proximity to this new art, as many artists ensured would be the case.

Theatres remained the center of Theatre, an art form which has traditionally been located in theatres. Official figures relating to the Theatre have not been published; it is therefore hard to know whether there are any figures or whether those responsible just don't care.

That being said, several Books were published in this and many, if not most, other countries. A tiny fraction of them were good and they were made almost entirely of paper. In the world of music, a similar good-to-bad ratio was observed. Music could be heard in the background on many television broadcasts, either on purpose or by accident. In some instances, music could be heard in the foreground. Many musicians worked on new projects, some worked on old projects, and a small number of them died, either peacefully or peacelessly.

WAR

As we know, the wars have occupied several column inches in the newspapers and indeed on-screen. This year, the countries which previously were fighting have kept fighting, in some cases to a lesser degree. Huge numbers of people have died and/or become injured in the places in which the wars have been taking place. A vast majority of those people suffered as a direct or indirect result of those very wars—an observation in keeping with the patterns hitherto observed. Some of the wars are illegal. Many who are living in the places where the wars are not happening have voiced their disapproval, or at the very least appropriated the disapproval of a vocal majority and given it a go.

CELEBRITIES

What a year for the celebrities, nude and otherwise! If you were a celebrity this year, it was quite likely a prudent career move. If you were a nude celebrity, even better! Celebrity was the place to be seen. Sadly, many of them ceased to be either famous or alive. You won't remember all of them or recall their demises, but they were here when the year began and you have outlasted them against the odds.

What were the biggest celebrity moments this year? Who can say? That awards ceremony is surely a contender (remember the clothes thing? and the mistake?). Perhaps your celebrity highlight was one of the hairstyles (which were typical both in number and position)? Or one of the romantic entanglements (which were typical both in number and position)? Whatever your angle, the celebrities continued this year, and boy were we glad in some cases that they did! The most popular ways of enjoying them were:

1. Videos
2. Magazines
3. Television
4. Hiding in the bush
5. The Online

THE ONLINE

Were you on the Online this year? If not, you missed all of it! Not to worry; much of it is still there in the place it happened, and in many cases in other places too. If you see something that looks the same as another thing on the Online, you can be sure that at least one of them is not the original and was put there by someone who didn't actually make it. There were some major topics exciting people throughout the year, but it's extremely difficult to recall the vast majority of them, aside from the ones we're excited about right now.

This year, we have interacted on the Online in a manner befitting our mood, circumstance, and understanding. Those who have been elsewhere have been heavily critical of Online communications. The non-Online, or Nonline, continue to exhibit ignorance, jealousy, and decrepitude. Sadly for them, this year has been just as Online as previous ones. It's a drama fit for the television!

TELEVISION

A remarkable feature of this year's television programming was its similarity to last year's. If we could have predicted one trend in the media at the beginning of the year, it would have been Different Television. Regrettably, as the days turned into weeks and the weeks turned into months, it became apparent that we were in for another year of what we had already experienced, albeit in a different permutation and under another name. We were treated to the beginning of yet another show—yes, THAT one. The one we knew would finish finally did. Another one, which finished unexpectedly because of the event that happened relating to its cast, will no longer be broadcast as a new show but instead will be rebroadcast in the future in the order to which we're accustomed, starting at the start. Bafflingly, the other one, which could have ended quite some time ago but kept going due to a host of mysterious reasons, is still happening. Several new shows used the central ideas of a number of successful shows from the past, which guaranteed their success—an excellent idea that has proven itself time and time again, and which we expect to be used with greater frequency in the coming year.

Many believed that we would begin to watch televisions in a different way this year, but as it turned out, we're still using the eye method. In the coming year, many television viewers can expect to be using their retinas, neurons, and synapses; don't trade them in just yet. However, advances in online technology have enabled us to absorb television at an incredible speed using synopses.

Surely the Big Smoke started in the sticks?

•

Debbie Did Dallas One Time, You Guys,
Can We Just Please Move On, Nobody's Perfect

•

I wandered lonely as a Neptunian smell cube.

•

Who took the dang out of the ramalamadingdangdong?

•

When Nureyev was asked what his favorite position
in ballet was, he repliéed.

•

Run like the wind!
(Erratically and in the air.)

•

I like to unwind by carving pentagrams
on balloons with a chainsaw.

•

If you "hold these truths to be self-evident," why list them?!

•

"Relations"? "Relatives"?
It's six of one and half a cousin of the mother.

•

Scrotum: strong concept, poor execution

•

If Hitler had just had a thumb, things might have been different.

•

I only eat *Playboy* for the articles.

•

Did Elvis Costello ever finish that book?

•

When turtles retract their legs,
maybe they swap them around, just to keep it real.

•

Some men are traffic islands.

•

"The power of trikes propels you!"
—*The Exorcist* for kids

•

Manicurists are the most persistent file-sharers.

•

NEWSFLASH:
Meatloaf Now Willing to "Do That"

•

Who died and made you kin?

DID YOU MURDERED A GEESE?

turns on defendant, pointing finger
DID YOU MURDERED A GEESE?

stands in pond, points finger at frog
DID YOU MURDERED A GEESE?

looks in mirror, pointing at reflection
DID YOU MURDERED A GEESE?

extends telescope into drainpipe
DID YOU MURDERED A GEESE?

kneels beside ant, pointing at ant
DID YOU MURDERED A GEESE?

descends on a string from the cathedral rafters
DID YOU MURDERED A GEESE?

stares at corn flakes
DID YOU MURDERED A GEESE?

looks up at helicopter
DID YOU MURDERED A GEESE?

listens to mound of cocaine
DID YOU MURDERED A GEESE?

wanders into retirement party, pulls the plug on the music
DID YOU MURDERED A GEESE?

unwraps burrito
DID YOU MURDERED A GEESE?

mishears burp
DID YOU MURDERED A GEESE?

calls Kris Kristofferson on burger phone
DID YOU MURDERED A GEESE?

slaps fish with a leaf
DID YOU MURDERED A GEESE?

*tumbles into basement, turns the light on, leans toward laundry
basket with hands on hips*
DID YOU MURDERED A GEESE?

puts on Phil Collins mask
marches through Starbucks
DID YOU MURDERED A GEESE?

scrambles out of a cake
DID YOU MURDERED A GEESE?

interrupts political rally
DID YOU MURDERED A GEESE?

falls through ceiling onto dinner table
points at family
DID YOU MURDERED A GEESE?

climbs onto elephant
DID YOU MURDERED A GEESE?

pins bee to garage wall
DID YOU MURDERED A GEESE?

clears dancefloor during "Rock the Boat"
points at everyone in turn
DID YOU MURDERED A GEESE?

writes novel
throws novel on the floor
points at novel
DID YOU MURDERED A GEESE?

recording backing vocals for Lionel Richie
DID YOU MURDERED A GEESE?

emerges from mine shaft in rescue pod
shines torch into mine shaft
DID YOU MURDERED A GEESE?

shouts into Dictaphone
DID YOU MURDERED A GEESE?
puts Dictaphone in bottle, floats it out to sea

stares at moon
DID YOU MURDERED A GEESE?

pauses ocean documentary
points at sea cucumber
DID YOU MURDERED A GEESE?

tunnels into U.N. Security Council chamber
DID YOU MURDERED A GEESE?

follows a Slinky down the stairs
DID YOU MURDERED A GEESE?

points microphone at spider
DID YOU MURDERED A GEESE?

builds snowman
DID YOU MURDERED A GEESE?

*emerges from prop foliage during production of A *Midsummer Night's Dream**
points at front row
DID YOU MURDERED A GEESE?

shouts at Natural History Museum
DID YOU MURDERED A GEESE?

meditates with the Dalai Lama
opens one eye
DID YOU MURDERED A GEESE?

starts shaving beard
looks at razor
DID YOU MURDERED A GEESE?

emerges from tear in the seat of MC Hammer's pants
DID YOU MURDERED A GEESE?

lifts rocks, points at bugs
DID YOU MURDERED A GEESE?

stops Road Runner with a giant mirror
DID YOU MURDERED A GEESE?

chases Mario along Rainbow Road
DID YOU MURDERED A GEESE?

opens Russian nesting dolls
DID YOU MURDERED A GEESE?
DID YOU MURDERED A GEESE?
DID YOU MURDERED A GEESE?
DID YOU MURDERED A GEESE?

dances erratically around handbag
DID YOU MURDERED A GEESE?

phones self
DID YOU MURDERED A GEESE?
NO I NOT MURDERED A GEESE

hacks through wardrobe with hatchet
reaches Narnia
prods signpost with finger
DID YOU MURDERED A GEESE?

studies rainbow
focuses on indigo
DID YOU MURDERED A GEESE?

kneels before a dead geese, shakes head
turns to see a geese smoking in the shadows
geese fades into shadows
YOU MURDERED A GEESE!

If there's a better sleeves song than "Greensleeves,"
I have yet to hear it.

•

Trying to tell a joke at a party is like standing on a boat,
proposing to a stranger who's bungee jumping overhead.

•

My 5-year plan
2017: famuos
2018: go to moon
2019: bring back moon
2020: friend with ryan gosleng
2021: fly away with him on moon

•

Had I the heavens' embroidered cloths,
I'd sell them down at the market and buy a space suit.

•

If a hipster uses a trouser press, he's just being ironic.

•

"LAMENT OF THE INEPT EGYPTOLOGISTS"
Sarcophagus
Ontopofus.
Get this sarcophagus
Offofus.

•

10 Things I Hate About 10 Things I Hate About You would be a
better film than *10 Things I Hate About You*, which I hate.

•

How to Levitate:
1. Find an idiot

•

The thigh bone's connected to the cheek bone. Total disaster.

•

I'm nothing if not.

•

As usual, there was nothing of interest at the end of the plank.

•

For every election there is an equal and opposite re-election.

•

Doctor? Hello. Sorry to bother you, but it's pretty serious:
The present keeps pushing me further away from the past.
Yes, I'll hold.

•

Here's a review of me: I am the best.

SWIMITAR

Don't bother putting makeup and
fancy stilettos on your calculator.
It's what's inside that counts.

·

The Beatles will never forget that time when my band played
on top of The Beatles on top of a building.

·

The flimsiest book I ever read was a pauperback hovel.

·

Did you ever look up at a plane in the sky and think, "I wish I
could buy something from the in-flight magazine right now"?

•

Directing a road safety advertisement?
Just instruct the actor to visualize a wall
getting really big, really quickly.

•

Nerdiest pop song? "It's the Countdown Final."

•

I'm not sure drunken semaphore sends out the right signals.

•

Tip: Write all your secrets on shredded paper,
thus saving time on shredding.

•

How do you solve a problem like diarrhea?

•

"I just ran over a dog!"
—a flea

•

What goes "KNOCK knock KNOCK knock KNOCK knock"?
A knock-knock joke in a washing machine.

•

The best thing about being a pirate
is getting to kill anyone who sees you crying.

•

If I had Brad Pitt's face,
I'd wonder where the rest of his body was.

•

A duck's bark never echoes.

•

Sometimes I just like to go home and play in my guitar.

•

You've got to speciate to accumulate.

INSTRUCTIONS

1. Put a shoelace in your mouth.
2. Walk onstage.
3. Wait for silence.
4. Slowly pull the shoelace out through your eye socket.

1. Go to McDonald's.
2. Ask for the "Leonard Nimoy."
3. When they say they don't have a "Leonard Nimoy," stand on the counter and scream.

1. Dip the quill in the ink.
2. Take it out.
3. Dip your finger in the ink.
4. Leave it in.

1. Choose a picnic spot.
2. Lay down your blanket.
3. Unpack the forks, the plates, and the flask of tea.
4. Moonwalk into the lake.

1. Get a puppy.
2. Become best friends.
3. Go on adventures together in a spaceship.
4. High-five everyone in the universe.
5. Die.

1. Turn on the Backwards Machine.
2. Put glass in the machine.
3. Take out the handful of sand that emerges.
4. Put sand in the machine.

1. Do a fake sneeze.
2. Elongate it so it turns into a long note.
3. Modulate it so you sound like an ambulance.
4. Do the Doppler effect.

1. Sit in a wok.
2. Hurtle down the mountainside.
3. When you reach the bottom, keep going.
4. Burrow into the earth.
5. Become a worm.

1. Bake a big cake.
2. Take off your socks and put your feet in the cake.
3. Happy birthday.

1. Shrink yourself to the size of an ant.
2. Enlarge your feet to human size.
3. Run around in the park.

1. Get published.
2. Become rich and famous.
3. Spend all your cash on mince.
4. Give the press an anonymous tip about your "mince room."

1. Put a miniature CCTV camera in a sprig of mistletoe.
2. Hang it up in the office.
3. Stand underneath and kiss the berries for 8 hours.

1. Get in the time machine.
2. Set it to "three seconds ago."
3. See 1.

1. Win the lottery.
2. Withdraw all of your winnings.
3. Next week, enter every single combination you can afford.
4. Lose the lottery.

1. Find cave.
2. Walk in.
3. Keep going.
4. Avoid rock.
5. Ignore bruise.
6. Turn corner.
7. Fall into hole.
8. Bleed to death.

1. Await instructions.
2.

"We'll always have Paris!"
—couple who abducted Paris

•

Teach a man to fish,
he'll still need vegetables and grains for a balanced diet.

•

"Say it, don't spray it!"
—man who's been dating the ocean
for longer than he'd planned

•

I didn't get where I am today—I was constructed from the
ground up by caterpillars with hammers.

•

In the olden days, a mash-up usually consisted of a yodeler crashing through the roof of a chamber music rehearsal.

•

Whenever I catch someone staring at my penis, I look at it and say, "MINE'S bigger than THAT."

•

The "common heat." There's your cure.

•

Turns out I'm allergic to that food I hate. Typical!

•

Overheard in the singles bar on the Enterprise: "I'm a Kirk rash survivor."

•

"I remember when this was nothing but Yields." —future person getting nostalgic for roads

•

Thinking of having kids? Call them "Johnifitsaboy" and "Maryifitsagirl."

•

I wouldn't say I stayed up too late at last night's
post-conference orgy, but I felt a little delegate this morning.

•

1. catch a swallow
2. swallow a mint
3. mint a coin
4. coin a phrase
5. phrase a question
6. question a suspect
7. suspect a friend

•

If you want my body and you think I'm sexy
and you like Legos and you own socks and you eat food
and you have a name, I forget what I was saying.

•

I woke up this morning. Beat that, dinosaurs!

•

"What is the deal with helicopter food?"
—corporate stand-up

•

Remember that scene in *Titanic* where they all spin-danced so hard that forty-seven poor people flew off into the ocean?

•

There's no excuse for eating the dog's homework.

•

Babies shouldn't smoke. Why is nobody saying this?
I feel like I'm going crazy here.

•

He lifted up his dong to reveal another dong.
He lifted up the second dong to reveal a third.
It was just dong after dong. Excessive.

•

I want to build a flotation tank
in which other flotation tanks can relax.

•

Showering during a thunderstorm is amazing!
But I was soon asked to leave the helipad.

•

A POEM
babies love boobies
puppies love poopies

•

The only time I have a lifejacket is when
I'm in the sky. Makes you think

•

Mr. Gorbachev, build me a patio.

•

HOW YOUR HOUSE WORKS:
- Spiders eat the flies
- Dust mites eat flakes of your skin
- Cockroaches lay eggs in your ears while you sleep

THE SWAMP

Nobody in this swamp is happy, Charles.
We built the swamp wrong.

I'm not happy in this swamp, Dolores.
I'm not happy about this entire swamp situation.

Do you think the others are happy in the swamp, Esther?
I'm looking over at them right now and they don't look happy.
Genuinely. Look at them, over there.

Should we be happier, Sylvia?
In this swamp?
Could we be?
Perhaps it's the swamp that's making us unhappy.

What went wrong with the swamp, Joseph?
Was it the location?
Was it the ambience?
Was it us?

Bernard, this swamp isn't working for me.
Is there anything we can do about the swamp?
From within?
A committee, maybe?

Terry, remember what it was like?
Before we came here to the swamp?
Wasn't it grand? It was, Terry. It was.
Could it ever be the same again?

I'm telling you, Leanne, we're in the wrong damn swamp.
I'm convinced there's a better swamp a couple of miles down
the road.

I mean, this is a perfect example, Jerry.
Jerry. Are you listening? Okay.
Well, see here, the furniture is submerged.
In the swamp, yes.

How about it, Muriel?
How about we just leave the swamp?

Sure, we'll need to pack first, that'll take a while.
But consider the alternative.

This swamp has come between us, Edward.
Literally. I can't even jump to your log anymore.
We used to be so carefree, never worried about where our patio had gone.

Tell me this, Bill:
Other than the view, what does this swamp actually have going for it?
Also, have you seen my bicycle?
Don't tell me it's——?

Pat, this is an awful, awful swamp.
I know I have nothing to compare it to, but still.
Maybe we didn't pay attention when we moved in.
Maybe we were blinded by love.
Maybe.

This is just great. I'm lodged in the swamp, Lou. I hope you're happy.

Public erections are controvertical.

•

I hate being the last to eat from the collection plate.

•

Does a child's upbringing influence its adult life?
Parently so.

•

If a ghost introduces itself by saying "I'm a ghost,"
it's not a real ghost and you should demand a refund.

•

spins globe
so THAT'S how mother fell off

•

World War II was at its best in the years prior to it.

•

The most evil singer is Robert Sith.

•

"If there's a way to tell the difference between
crayons, I've yet to hear about it."
—man who has gone blind and strange from eating crayons

•

"It's raining, men. Hallelujah."
—Noah, to his sons

•

They've removed Algeria. Someone just removed it recently.
Not sure if a committee or whatever. Awful news.

•

My local school has a huge outsider art collection.

•

There's a very real possibility that they froze my good brain.

•

The party in my pants was too noisy, so I called the police.

•

TOP KEYBOARD SHORTCUTS:
1. Ctrl-Ctrl: Nothing
2. AltGr-Ctrl-Alt-Ctrl: Nothing
3. Alt-Alt: Nothing
4. Cut through woods to reach keyboard

•

:In thewar on langridge, spleling was fist too go
~~then puncuation

•

"Exit, pursuing a human."
—Shakespeare for bears

•

Thought for the day: Count to 86,400 seconds.

DINOSAURS OF THE FUTURE

#3

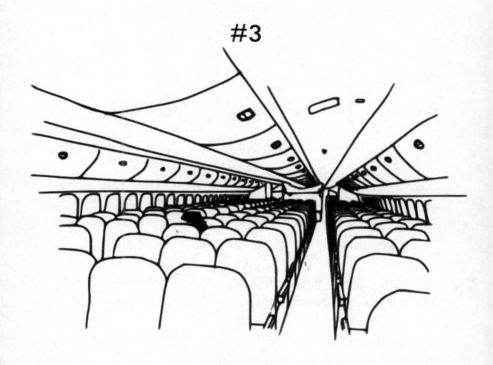

Flying dinosaur

BAD AIR DAY

Suddenly discovered I'm allergic to air.

I can't touch that, it's covered in air.

I think I got some air on my sleeve. Wipe it off, please, just use a towel or something. Quick! I can't have any air on me!

Yeah, I suppose I'm kinda hungry, but does the sandwich have air in it? Really? Then no thanks. I can't eat it if there's air in it.

I'm pretty sure I can smell air in this room. This is freaking me out. I cannot be in the same room as air!

Please tell me you're not eating meat that has air in it?

I think I just saw some air. Ran out of the house and locked the door just in case.

That which does not call me makes me a stranger.

•

Sir, could you step loudly out of the vehicle please?
Sir, is this your clown car?
Sir, I'm going to need you to blow into this balloon.

•

When at sea, I have a tremendous sense of whale-baying.

•

Rave reviews are usually very positive, because of the drugs.

•

Hippie Commune "Decimated" Following Rocket Launch:
Rockets, disguised as trees, activated when hugged;
hippies now en route to Middle East

•

Cher reminds me of a young Cher.

•

If I had a catapult, I would catapult a bookshelf at the moon
so that the children of the future could learn.

•

Buster Keaton's favorite genre was silence fiction.

•

I forgot to enter the Olympics.
All that upper-right body strength for nothing.

•

I ate food in college, but I didn't inhale.

•

I was not on the farm when the animals burst.

•

If you're shooting fish in a barrel,
I suggest getting out of the barrel first.

•

If you look at a shoe for long enough, you'll miss your train.

•

"I came as soon as I heard."
—obscene caller

•

I cut off my nose to spite my nose.

INTERVAL TWO: MOTIVATIONAL SPEECH

Attention, you! We're on the other side now! You need to sit up and behave yourself! Get a grip on your computer screen! Quit gargling! Put down the crack hose! Clean out your ears! Unhand your junk! Look up from that pornography manual! Shut your yap! Listen to my typing! Stop scratching that! Hear me now! Abandon that debate! Ignore the wasp! Hurry up and finish that fart! Focus on the words! Hush your face! Don't answer the phone! Sit like you mean it! I have things you need to experience! You are a guinea pig! There will be a questionnaire! Clear your throat if you must! Then no more noises! Concentrate or be left behind! Throw that magazine at the wall! There is only one path! Lick those crumbs from around your mouth! Fix your tie! Stop trying to identify that smell! Breathe less ignorantly! Think harder! Drink my sentences! Slurp the syllables! You no longer care about that other thing you were doing! There's a pube on your thigh! Forget it! You may blink now! Now stop blinking! Stop frowning like that! You can probably keep up if you raise your game! There's juice on your chin! Don't feel bad about your inferiority! Feel bad about my superiority! You'd better be taking notes! This horse don't stop! Don't look away! Fight the urge to urinate! Think about your decisions! Slap yourself if drooping! Acknowledge my skills! Your buttocks are not really sore! Stand up and walk around your chair! Cry briefly to purge stupidity! Congratulate yourself on this minor breakthrough! Now sit down! Dig into the wordmud! Jetski on my majestic flow! Remember the following keywords: panpipes, trammelled, ablutions, yelp! Study harder! Strap yourself to my houseboat! We're going upriver! I'll use you to scoop up fish! These are new times! This is your golden ticket! Smile! This is no time for reflection! There is only onward! Don't let your bowels get the better of you! You're under my tutelage now! Step up! Suck in your belly! There are things to be done! We have an important meeting on the top floor! There'll be pretzels! Act like you've slept! Spit out that chewing gum! Get that ridiculous song out of your head! Don't mess this up! Reconsider that haircut! Tuck in your folds! Wash your armpits! This is a heavy experience! Maybe you shouldn't persevere with that outfit! Eyes on me! No slacking! Look sharp! Blow your nose on whatever's near! Do some stretches! You are currently at 9%! Now pretend to be a motorbike! Not in an ironic way! Louder! Don't waste my time with substandard vehicle impressions! You're still on the lowest rung! I should throw prawns at you! Show me dignity! You didn't make the grade! You weren't concentrating enough! Hang your head! I ought to kick your ass through a wet tunnel! I'm sleepy now!

Once in a while, a pendulum pauses to fart.

•

Threw the looking glass; was escorted from the shop.

•

If you ever get caught red-handed, pull your trousers down and reach into a cookie jar—nobody will believe the story.

•

RECIPE
Ingredients:
- 2 ingredients
- 5 units of ingredient
- ingredient powder

Directions:
Mix ingredients and ingredient powder. Agitate.

•

Sometimes when I ask the shopkeeper for a scratch card,
what I really want is a hug.

•

You don't like my pentameter, you say?
Well, I prefer iambic. That okay?

•

No and Please are my outer names.

•

The Larry Sanders Show should have been called
Handling Shandling.

•

The Monkey Theorem:
A monkey typing the Complete Works of Shakespeare
would eventually hit keys at random.

•

"I remember when all of this was just an enormous hover-city!"
—confused time-traveller

•

Why don't cookery shows end with
"And then, turn off the oven"?
Irresponsible, if you ask me.

•

How to Spot a Trainspotter
1. Disguise yourself as a choo-choo.
2. Make a choo-choo noise.
3. Keep going, good job.

•

You fill up my senses like a night in a forest!
(You're terrifying, hard to see, texturally confusing, cold
and damp, and you smell like wet leaves.)

DISCARDED STAR WARS FANFIC IDEAS

We clawed through the rubble for what seemed like hours. The place was very untidy indeed. My assistant, Sulu, began to s

"There's been a robbery!" These were not my words, but the words of a PoliceBot, who had burst into my detective office w

Captain Picard stood on the top of the space shuttle and disrobed. His companion, a friendly robot called Data, cooked a

The Doctor stepped out of his moon buggy. His muscles twitched. There was a Romulan nearby! But where? He used his psychi

The jewelry market exploded in an explosion of yellows and oranges. The year was 2328! The aliens had landed. "Mr. Pres

He couldn't get in. It was because of the door. He told me to open the door. But I couldn't. You see . . . . I myself am a door

The tall man looked out of the rectangular window at the dark space. Several stars were fighting. There were guns and everyth

"Coffee?" I turned around. It was my pet android, Andrew Android. She was suggesting a hot beverage. I declined. My cold testic

Somebody's gonna pay for this, she told herself. With Space Money. She walked away from the exploding moon, angry about

Nefertiti, my ostrich, never once stopped complaining all the way to the supermarket. I said, "I'll leave you in space if you're not

Rain splattered the window. And the rest of the house. There was so much rain on this planet, thought Martin. Little did he kn

Unbuttoning his blouse, Spacelieutenant Horns blinked away a tear. He hadn't signed up for this. In fact, he couldn't even writ

The stars were, by now, just hurling globs of hot stuff at each other. "We should probably step back," thought Joe. But curiosity got

Michael Jackson albums reviewed:
Off the Wall: invincible
Thriller: off the wall
Bad: thriller
Dangerous: bad
Invincible: dangerous

•

I'm sure kids see me as a fatter figure.

•

Does the body rule the mind or does the mind rule the body
or is there a lemur somewhere with a remote control?

•

"If it's a human head, we've got it!"
—local human head superstore slogan

•

I couldn't begin to tell you how hesitant I am.

•

The best number of times to be born is 1.

•

Butterflies need to be educated
about the consequences of their actions.

•

In the Bosch painting of my life,
the Internet would be the rectal flute.

•

Knowledge is the root of all superknowledge.

•

Maybe I'll arrange my books so that they're
stored inside one another like Russian dolls, decreasing
in pretentiousness as they get smaller.

•

WEATHER UPDATE:
The weather is at today's weather level.
There have been some temperatures and now there
is a current temperature.

•

People who live in glass houses shouldn't.

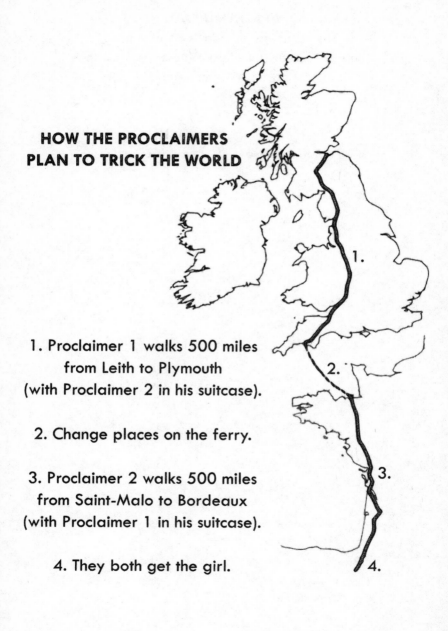

HOW THE PROCLAIMERS
PLAN TO TRICK THE WORLD

1. Proclaimer 1 walks 500 miles
from Leith to Plymouth
(with Proclaimer 2 in his suitcase).

2. Change places on the ferry.

3. Proclaimer 2 walks 500 miles
from Saint-Malo to Bordeaux
(with Proclaimer 1 in his suitcase).

4. They both get the girl.

A CONVERSATION

A: Morning!

B: Hi.

A: What's the matter?

B: I'm just . . . not feeling great at the moment.

A: Ah. Do you feel like a joke?

B: Yeah, okay. Why not.

A: What's the best way to mend a broken window?

B: I don't know. What's the best way to mend a broken window?

A: Probably ring a professional, I'd say. You want it done properly, you know?

B: What?

A: What do you call a monkey with no arms?

B: I don't know. What do you call it?

A: What kind of monkey is it? Big or small? I don't think monkey names should be too close to human names. They're more like pets, I think.

B: But you asked me . . .

A: How many pencils can you fit in a wigwam?

B: No idea.

A: That's a tough question, isn't it? It'd have to be at least 100,000. But you'd have to zip up the door first. Do we know someone with a wigwam? I'm sure we could find one pretty easily. What's the difference between a Christmas cake and a tricycle?

B: You can't eat a tricycle.

A: That's true. A man walks into a shop.

B: And?

A: Just a shop.

B: What?

A: Every morning at half past eight, like clockwork. Just walks into a shop.

B: And what happens?

A: Depends on what day it is, I suppose. He usually gets the newspaper, sometimes some milk, things like that. What do you get if you cross a snail with an onion?

B: I couldn't begin to imagine.

A: And what if the snail then walked away?

B: Snails don't walk.

A: Are you sure? They can't swim, though, can they? No, that's impossible. Forget about that. That's just confusing.

B: Yes, I agree.

A: What's the softest part of a tennis racket?

B: The strings?

A: No, I think there's a softer part. Something . . . think it begins with H or . . . nope, no, wait, is it K? Hmmm. I'll have to look it up. What's the loudest number?

B: Let me guess . . . number 2?

A: Hardly. Don't they get louder as they get bigger?

B: That's not what I meant.

A: Knock.

B: Who's there?

A: Hold on, wait a sec. Knock.

B: Who's there?

A: I meant knock, knock. Is that too many knocks? Never mind.

B: I'll try my best.

A: So, there are three men in a hotel.

B: Right. Go on.

A: No, is it a hotel? Yeah, okay, no, it's a hotel. And there are three of them. Men.

B: Wow.

A: So there they are, in a hotel, the hotel. And out walks a woman. Or she walks in, actually.

B: Is this relevant?

A: Oh, I'd imagine so. And the first man says, "Where did she go?"

B: So she walked out, not in.

A: Exactly. And the second man says, "Wasn't that my wife?"

B: Uh-huh.

A: I wonder where she went.

B: That's what I'm waiting to find out.

A: Should we wait for her to come back?

B: What, to the hotel? In the joke?

A: Yeah, you're right. It'd take too long.

Data from *Star Trek: The Next Generation* once
smuggled himself into the Glastonbury festival, one component
at a time, in hundreds of backpacks.

•

"Have you got a minute to talk about furniture?"
—Jesus goes door-to-door

•

I'd like to write a double entendre, but I don't have it in me.

•

Snail tourists:
you're never too far from a highway truck-stop mushroom.

•

A vegan is a human of milk-kindness.

•

My focus group was probably drunk.

•

Bungalows would be a lot more fun if
they were called bungungalows.

•

In heaven, everything is slightly cheaper;
all frozen foods are kept at 1987 prices.

•

Do hypothetical monkeys have supposable thumbs?

•

Once, just once, I'd like to see an elephant shoot a horse.

•

Would it be better or worse if elbows had kneecaps?

•

It's not the throwing my hands in the air that
I care about, but where they land.

•

The loudest type of mime is pantomime.

•

If you're having trouble getting onto a horse,
just pretend you were doing stretches.

•

When all is said and done, that's called the apocalypse.

•

Wet Wet Wet could have saved everybody a lot of time
by simply calling themselves Wet.

•

What have the Morons ever done for us?

HOW TO TELL IF YOU'RE
HAVING A NIGHTMARE

1. Are you trying to play the piccolo but every note sounds like a lion and then the piccolo is a lion?

2. Is it simultaneously 1985 and 1994 and there's a bear chasing you through a dusty warehouse?

3. Is there fondue everywhere except where it's meant to be?

4. Has the stranger you crushed with a rock in the burning forest reappeared, smiling and hovering?

5. Have your innards solidified and have you begun to emit regular beeps?

6. Is there a noise in the walls and it gets louder when you blink?

7. Have you been thinking about your buttocks?

8. Is there something moving in the background of that old photograph of the ruined mill?

9. When you dusted for prints, did the statue disintegrate, leaving a pile of sugar on the marble plinth?

10. Did the skeleton become larger the faster you ran, until you collided and the hot bones ground you down?

11. Is there a disjointed narrative, poor lighting, too many characters, 2 stars out of 5?

12. Is there no need for food, and you only stop running to tear strips of flesh from the cold earth?

13. Do you keep falling down the stairs and turning into another whorl of bones, but never breaking?

14. Do none of the place names make sense (e.g. Ominous Shadow Lane, Low Bass Throb, Bad Thing Area)?

15. 0001101010011001010010111100010100101110010000000110101 010100111010001?

16. Are you pregnant, but you can't be pregnant, you're a museum?

17. Are there bodies in the crawl space but you wrapped them in She-Ra blankets?

18. Is there nothing to eat but hot pencils?

19. Might you be a cockerel?

20. Are you your father and your son, and your father (you) is the son of your son (you), and your son (you) is the father of your father (you)?

21. Were there very few toilet breaks on the journey over the pink mountain?

22. Do your house and the beach share a basement?

23. Are you in a tree, covered in seaweed, trying to convince Dame Judi Dench to put her clothes back on and sing about lobsters?

24. Are you trying to punch a corpse but your arms feel like they're underwater?

25. Are you in the gizzard bucket but your claws have melted?

26. You can't

27. Are you in the maternity ward and a nightmare is emerging from between your legs?

28. BOO

If you're scared of flying in a plane, then don't even think about flying outside of a plane.

•

Worst wine: Vin D'iesel.

•

I do not like green eggs and anything.

•

A thought before bedtime: "I think I'll go to bed."

•

Scram if you want to go faster.

•

A hundred years ago, if the paparazzi
photographed you having an affair, you had to stay
in the same position for five minutes.

•

I'm very careful when it comes to putting on trousers.
Always legs first, then tail, then glue the whole thing shut.

•

Of all those much proudest of them things
that what me done, has have to said but all of me spellens
is those what did be the most bests.

•

I like to borrow a book from the library,
swap the first and last sentences, return the book,
wait until someone borrows it and kill them.

•

1. Stop
2. Find a notepad and pencil
3. Listen
4. Take notes
5. Brainstorm
6. Feedback
7. Toilet break

8. Biscuit
9. NOW collaborate

•

The punishment for crimes against rhyme is a garroted carotid.

•

Most popular song played in the bus on the way to boot camp:
"Road to No Hair."

•

I buy my weapons from a tomahawkonist.

•

Remember when Snickers was called Boothroyd's Tonic Biscuit?

•

Yesterday, I ate my dessert before my breakfast!
It was today's breakfast.

•

Bad birthday present: a robot that sweats.

•

This ain't no party! This ain't no disco!
This is a final year quantum mechanics examination
and I must ask you to leave.

•

I've had it up to here with people
who expect me to visualize how high their hands are.

•

The loudest bone in the body is the trombone.

•

If I've shot you in the face, it's only because
you were standing between me and my dreams,
which I was trying to shoot in the face.

•

Infinity is like if eight got really drunk and passed out.

HONK

HONK IF YOU'RE A JAZZ HAPPENING

HOONK IF YOU HAVE TOO MANY VOWELS

HONK IF PUPPIES

HONK IF YOU'RE EATING A LIVE CHICKEN

HONK IF YOU HAVE OPINIONS

HONK IF YOU SIMPLY CANNOT BELIEVE THE NEWS

HONK IF EVERYTHING SMELLS WEIRD

HONK IF YOU'RE RELEVANT

HONK IF YOU BOUGHT MUSCLES ON THE INTERNET

HONK IF YOU SUSPECT THAT RAINBOWS ARE A HOAX

HONK IF YOU'RE THE THIRD WHEEL IN AN IMAGINARY RELATIONSHIP

HONK IF THEY PUT A TRANSMITTER IN YOUR BRAIN

HONK

JUST HONK GODDAMMIT

MORE HONKS PLEASE

CAN I GET A HONK?

HONK LIMIT EXCEEDED

RECOMMENDED WORDS:
Splat
Fixins
Geschmuckas
Popsocks
Frippery
Pancreas
Thruppence
Onions
Whence
Burbles
Purple
Clop
Burst
Futtock
Pantaloons
Slurp
Plump

Muscling
Flump

•

If you catch a fish in polluted water,
is it right or wrong to throw it back in?

•

People always talk about the first rule of Fight Club,
but the second one is just as important.

•

"Hello! Is it me you're talking to?"
—Lionel Bickle

•

Cut out the middleman: pee on a jellyfish.

•

needle scratch
I still can't find a vein

•

To find your porn star name, just try to
remember the last place you put it.

'Tis better to have loved and lost and
found some pirate treasure and got to meet Elvis
and flown to Saturn than never to have loved at all.

•

People are strange when you're a strangler.

•

Dogs can't see ghosts; they just hate doors.

•

If you're afraid of underwater plants, SEA KELP!

•

BIGGEST-SELLING BOX SETS, 1876:
1. A Spinster's Country Walks
2. The New Caledonian Anthology
3. Ghent and Environs
4. Hot Fresh Murders

•

Still can't believe I won the Emmy for Outstanding Library Fines.

•

a youth frantically searches every inch of his school
Why can't I find a Dislike button?

•

I gave myself a badge for "Most Spare Badges."

•

If you must diddle your widdle, politely excuse yourself and
explain that you're going to "extinguish the flame of desire."

•

At the Dalai Lama's funeral,
Elton John is going to sing "Sandal in the Wind."

•

After I got through the hedge maze, I discovered to my dismay
that the next field was a Sudoku.

•

Shoe shops: Don't buy an expensive sign—
just hang a bag of drugs over your door.

•

The Million Dollar Question:
Why won't you give me a million dollars?

•

I took the second-last train to Clarksville
and eloped with the Monkees.

•

"Don't fence in me!"
—an angry gymnasium

INTERVAL THREE: THE HARD QUIZ

Quiz must be completed in less than more than 5 minutes.
Chalk pastels are allowed.
You may being now.

1. Calculate the height of Austria multiplied by its weight and express the result in kilogoujons. _____

2. My first is in sand, my second is in onions, my third is not in jail, and my fourth has one of my second. What is he? _____

3. In which year was the electrical hanging fluttertrundle invented? _____
A: 12
B: 19999
C: 002h7

4. Complete the following proverb: "Two knees ne'er clacked so hard in the folded breeches of _____."

5. If the spoon coefficient exceeds the ratio of knapsacks to eggs, how much grease is required to baste the horse?

_____

6. If a train lives in London at five o'clock and moves in a straight line for three hours, how long is the speed of it?

_____

11. True or false or otherwise: The silent ingredients in beer are starch, silt, jonathan, angerberry, and tuna hair. _____

8. One of these statements is less false than the other—which one? _____
A: "Six minus six squared"
C: "minus six squared plus"

9. What is that which is the that what not is which that was the this when that was not the who? (To the nearest 100) _____

10. If four cormorants enter the Venezuelan food store and five cormorants leave, how much food is in the cash register?

_____

All those attempting the Hard Quiz:

Pancils down. Close your calcinators.
Arms folded, wait for the invigilator to collect your papyrus.

If music be the food of love, it goes straight to the hipsters.

•

"Tell me about it, stump!"
—from the musical *Trease*

•

Hazelnuts: an excellent source of hazelnuts

•

Think of the children!
Now think of the children piloting
a zeppelin packed with explosives!
Now think of something else!

•

ACTIVATE COOL-O-METER

>USER, YOU ARE TOO COOL FOR:
[SCHOOL]
>COOL ENOUGH FOR:
[PRISON]
>NOT COOL ENOUGH FOR:
[CHAD'S PARTY ON SATURDAY]

•

Can't wait to be old and gray, sitting on the porch, reminiscing about my favorite TV shows from when I was a kid, like *Ultimate Acid Dragon Chronicles: Infinite Rainbow Apocalypse.*

•

On quiet days, Neptune spent hours
contemplating his narwhal.

•

DO YOU LIKE QUESTIONS?

YES: 46%
NO: 46%
WHAT?: Dads who weren't listening

A SNAIL'S DIARY

1997

New diary!
New pen!

1998

Lost family.
Sad

1999

~~Happy New~~
Happy ~~Ch~~ Xmas

2000

End of page!
New page!
Yes!

2001

Lost pen.
New pen.

2002

There's more page

2003

Found family.
Sad

A Strangler's Eulogy: "Dearly Begloved, . . ."

•

I saw a dam weeping uncontrollably. It was recently beavered.

•

History will indicate me.

•

I'm saving my best material for my deathbed.

wait hang on
FIVE
where's my lucky frog?
FOUR
i'm not leaving without him
THREE
let me off this thing
TWO
now dammit
ONE
dear god no
BLASTOFF

. . . .

Goodnight, moon!
Goodnight, voices!

. . . .

The dark side of the moon

is the man in the moon, mooning.

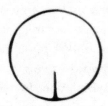

APPENDIX A

Oh, you made it to the back of the book? Excellent. Sorry, I was asleep.

So . . . it's time for me to come clean. I lied. There's nothing about me here.

There's nothing about me anywhere.

Who cares? You're far more interesting anyway.

Now tell me about You. Speak into the book.

Little bit louder. Louder. No, that was too loud. I think we're both embarrassed for you. Maybe just write on the page with your finger. The one you're not using to pick your nose.

First, write your name. (We're all friends here. I don't mind if you've got some wayward vowels, or a couple of consonants you're not proud of.) Then your favorite dinner. (I promise to cook it next time we have a sleepover!) And if you want to jot down your bank details, I'm not going to love you any less for that. Remember: no pen, pencil, marker, crayon, charcoal, or jam. This book's already lost 20% of its value through oxygen contact and people-touching. Let's not ruin it completely!

WRITEYBOX

Good, good. We're discovering each other. This is nice, isn't it? Who says books can't be interactive?

SPEAKYBOX

This is the Speakybox. The great thing about it is that you can use it over and over again. So if you change hobbies, or have some news, or need assistance, you can let me know.

Just open this page and shout into the Speakybox any time, day or night.

Now, friend, please use the Speakybox to list:

- Your birthday
- Your pets (include your first one)
- Your hobbies
- Any interesting names in your family (e.g., mother's maiden name)
- Your top holiday destinations
- A four-digit number that's close to your heart

APPENDIX B
James Thomas interviews James Thomas

Me: Thanks for agreeing to do this interview. I know you're busy.

Me: Sure, no problem. What magazine is this for?

Me: It's for Time Magazine Boobs Edition.

Me: Great. I have a subscription. So, what would you like to know?

Me: Well, let's start with your early life.

Me: Wait, is this interview set entirely in the past?

Me: Well, mostly.

Me: Okay. I can do this. How many things do you need me to remember?

Me: One per year? Or thereabouts. That okay?

Me: Fine with me. Do you want to know about the time I was born?

Me: Absolutely. Was it a positive experience?

Me: Being born was the most positive experience I had had up to that point. I couldn't remember a happier time.

Me: But wasn't your birth fraught with complications? Such as copyright issues and allegations of bribery?

Me: Lies.

Me: This is clearly a touchy subject.

Me: No, not at all. It's just that I hoped all of that was behind me. I've grown.

Me: Let's move on. It's fair to say that your childhood was full of incident.

Me: Oh yes. On a second-by-second basis.

Me: For example, your presidency.

Me: Yeah—due to an administrative error, I was president for exactly one second.

Me: Was there much paperwork involved?

Me: To be honest, I wasn't focused on paperwork back then. I was more hands-on.

Me: Did you meet anyone interesting in your time in office?

Me: There simply wasn't enough time to schmooze. Pity.

Me: Looking back, would you do things differently?

Me: Definitely. I would have gone to war with the Pacific Ocean.

Me: Really? Why the Pacific?

Me: Oh, it knows what it did.

Me: It's important to note that you were only six at the time.

Me: I wasn't ready for the presidency. I see that now.

Me: Was school a happy place for you?

Me: Not my own school, no. But I did get lost once and find another school.

Me: It says here that you excelled at sports.

Me: That's not for me to say. I mean, I did captain the computer team.

Me: Your school had a computer team?

Me: Not technically. I trained some computers to swim.

Me: Computers can swim?

Me: They can be taught the basics. You can lead them to water. They're allergic, I think.

Me: Did you make many friends in school?

Me: What do you mean by that?

Me: Well, I just—are you angry?

Me: Maybe.

Me: Well, it's a simple question. Did you or did you not have friends in school?

Me: I can't entirely recall.

Me: You can't recall having any friends?

Me: Well, I do remember playing Russian roulette with the school counselor.

Me: Tell me about the shooting.

Me: How did you know about that? Man, the shooting. Yeah, I shot a balloon dog.

Me: But why would you shoot a balloon dog?

Me: I was aiming for the clown.

Me: What have you got against clowns?

Me: Nothing whatsoever. But this one owed me money. We had a lemonade stand.

Me: Can we talk about the time you disappeared at the age of twelve?

Me: Yes, those were the longest three years of my life.

Me: What happened? You've mentioned aliens before.

Me: Yes. I was kidnapped and forced to watch *Aliens* for three years.

Me: That must have been . . . challenging.

Me: I can't begin to imagine what I must have felt.

Me: Wow. So who were the kidnappers?

Me: They never showed their faces. Turns out it was the old computer team.

Me: What did they want?

Me: They wanted to make me watch *Aliens* for three years.

Me: That's all?

Me: They're ruthless.

Me: How did the ordeal end?

Me: The TV broke. I think they were torturing both of us.

Me: When you re-entered society, had you changed?

Me: For a while, I only spoke in snatches of dialogue from *Aliens*.

Me: Did you feel like an outsider?

Me: No more than any other fifteen year old. But I thought it was the twenty-second century.

Me: How did that affect your relationships?

Me: I thought every bedroom was an egg chamber. In a way, I was right.

Me: Did it take long to recover?

Me: Years. I only got my first job—fireman—through overzealous hose-wielding.

Me: You have said that you were only ever truly comfortable as a fireman. Why's that?

Me: The anti-thermal underwear.

Me: You must have seen your fair share of suffering.

Me: Honestly, no. I generally fainted when we reached the fire.

Me: Have you had many jobs since then?

Me: Sure. Dog painter, pencil tester, astronaut, musicianist, nude model.

Me: Hang on—you were a nude model?

Me: Yes, at a school for the blind.

Me: You've lived such a full life. Except for those three years when you were kidnapped. What's left to achieve?

Me: Pi.

Me: How do you "achieve Pi"?

Me: I plan to achieve Pi in all aspects of my life. It guides me in all I do.

Me: Such as?

Me: I turn around Pi times before I go to sleep. I eat Pi kilograms of food each day. I have Pi friends.

Me: And can you recite Pi?

Me. Oh no. I refuse to do so on principle; I only permit myself to learn Pi things each day.

Me: Some quick questions before we finish. What's your proudest moment?

Me: 1988.

Me: Dream dinner party guests?

Me: A dozen clones of Henry VIII and the real one. I'd eat one every five minutes. Hey, it's my dream—my rules.

Me: Any final words?

Me: Stop looking at me like that.

Interview by James Thomas.
Thanks to James Thomas for being so generous with his time.

APPENDIX C
Questionnaire

Thank you for doing this.
Be sure to write each answer on or in
the appropriate box or line.

Name: □

Age: _____

    5. Do you find it stressful to complete questionnaires?

How do you cope with multiple-choice questions?

                                     a) very well □

                           b) well to very well □

c) well □

                d) reasonably well to well □

            e) reasonably well □

f) not very well to well □

               g) not very well □

      h) badly to not very well □

i) badly □

j) extremely badly to badly □

k) extremely   badly □

6. Do you worry if you can't quite find the right answer?

ye's □

yos □

not yes' □

not really

1. Are you easily **frightened?**

yes □

yes □

yes □

yes □

yes □

look behind you □

Address: □

ACKNOWLEDGMENTS

I have a lot of thanks, and I hope I remember them all.

Michelle, thank you for putting up with several years of this ridiculousness. You have the patience of a saint. Best wife ever.

This book wouldn't have seen the light of day without Natalie Galustian, the best agent in the whole wide world and one of the most amazing people I've ever met. Natalie, thanks a million for everything you've done for me and I will now become extremely famous and do you proud. Thanks also to the very lovely David Headley and all at DHH Literary Agency, with which I'm immensely proud to be associated.

Courtney Littler is my wonderful editor at St. Martin's Press. If it weren't for her, you wouldn't have a book to read right now. You'd be staring at your hands in a bookshop, instead of reading this. Reading your hands. Terrible. Thanks, Courtney, for being so encouraging, enthusiastic, and easy to work with—and, of course, for taking a chance on me. Furthermore, big thankses to David Curtis, who designed the cover, which I love to bits; to Anna Gorovoy, who designed the interior pages, making the whole thing pop; and to Andrea Serra, who copyedited the heck out of my gibberish. St. Martin's Press, you have been lovely.

To my family: thank you all for being my family and not someone else's, which, in my opinion, would be terribly confusing. You have always supported me in all my nonsenses, and I hope this one was worth it. There's more to come. I love you guys.

I'd also like to thank Graham Linehan for his support through the years, for showing an interest in what I do and for making me want to write. To Limmy: thank you, not only for the use of your image, but also for showing me how to harness an overactive mind. Jack Handey, you are an inspiration and a gentleman; your generosity is humbling. Thanks so much to Emma Allen and all at the *New Yorker* for giving me a platform I'm still not sure I deserve. Andrea Mann also, for the *Huffington Post* gig; big ups.

To all those who have followed me on Twitter: thanks. That has led to this. I won't let you down. To everyone who has supported *Crimer Show*: thank you for putting me on the map. To those who hate this book: you don't know the half of it. You should see the stuff I left out.

To my friends: you're the best. Thanks for that.

These also helped: tea, disco, BBC4.

Thanks also to anyone I've left out, and sorry to anyone I accidentally put in.

Finally, I would like to thank the Emperor of the Moon, for being my nemesis when I needed it the most. Our mutual hatred gives me the energy I need to face each day. But let me make one thing clear: when the moment is right, I will vanquish you and seize your throne, you filthy snake. Every night, I sharpen my sword, and I point it at the sky and howl. Your days are numbered.

INDEX